Pandemic Influenza Planning:
Information for Schools and Centers

Garry Wade McGiboney, Ph.D.

REVELTREE PUBLISHING COMPANY

Library of Congress Cataloging Service

Print ISBN 978-0-692-75692-8

Library ISBN 0692756922

First Edition by Garry McGiboney 2016

Pandemic Influenza Planning:
Information for Schools and Centers

Published by Reveltree Publishing Company

An imprint of the Reveltree Publishing Group

Cover Image: Designed by Reveltree Designers

Planning for Schools and Centers

Other Books by Garry McGiboney, Ph.D.

Crisis Management Planning for Schools and Centers

Lessons for Leaders and Governing Boards

The Private Side of Public Education

The Psychology of School Climate

When Darkness Finds Light

Planning for Schools and Centers

Acknowledgements

This book is dedicated to the loyal educators, first responders, and public health officials and workers who ensure that schools and communities are safe and are prepared for public health emergencies, including pandemics and epidemics.

All proceeds from the sale and purchase of this book will go to the Georgia Foundation Partnership for Public Education.

TABLE OF CONTENTS

Introduction

Epidemic and Pandemic

Public health authorities conclude the probability of an influenza pandemic has increased markedly in recent years, but an epidemic is more likely. A distinction should be made between an epidemic and a pandemic even though planning for each should overlap.

According to the Centers for Disease Control (CDC), an epidemic is a contagious, infectious or viral illness that spreads between and among people in one specific geographic region, such as a state, county, or even contained within a country without spreading beyond the borders.

A pandemic, according to the World Health Organization (WHO), differs significantly from an epidemic. Similar to an epidemic, a pandemic refers to a contagious, infectious or viral illness that spreads, but unlike an epidemic, a pandemic is not limited to one specific geographic region. A pandemic spreads across many countries and has the potential to spread worldwide and infect millions of people.

Seasonal Influenza and Pandemic Influenza

Seasonal flu is common in many countries, including the United States. Typically, in the United States the "flu season" begins in October, peaks in December, and lasts until March or April of the following year. The seasonal flu death rate varies considerably and contrary to popular belief, there are no reliable figures on the number of seasonal flu deaths in the United States. The CDC explains why:

> *CDC does not know exactly how many people die from seasonal flu each year. There are several reasons for this. First, states are not required to report individual seasonal flu cases or deaths of people older than 18 years of age to CDC. Second, seasonal influenza is infrequently listed on death certificates of people who die from flu-related complications. Third, many seasonal flu-related deaths occur one or two weeks after a person's initial infection, either because the person may develop a secondary bacterial co-infection (such as bacterial pneumonia) or because seasonal influenza can aggravate an existing chronic illness (such as congestive heart failure or chronic obstructive pulmonary disease). Also, most people who die from seasonal flu-related complications are not tested for flu, or they seek medical care later in their illness*

when seasonal influenza can no longer be detected from respiratory samples.

Despite the problems identifying an accurate number of seasonal deaths, CDC provides an estimate of seasonal flu deaths primarily for the purpose of informing citizens about the dangers of seasonal flu and the importance of flu vaccinations. Also, the estimates are essential in tracking the types of flu and the level of danger. For example, CDC reports that the death rate predictions for Influenza A H3N2 were more than double that of Influenza A H1N1.

The one exception to the lack of mandatory reporting of seasonal flu deaths is the reporting of children's death from seasonal flu. Beginning in 2004, flu deaths in children were made nationally notifiable through the Influenza Associated Pediatric Mortality Surveillance System.

Pandemic flu events do not occur annually and they are not common types of flu as is found in most seasonal flu viruses. A pandemic flu virus is almost always caused by a new virus or a mutation of a common flu virus, typically it is an influenza A strain that has mutated from a strain that infected an animal, most commonly birds or pigs. A pandemic flu event occurs approximately every 20-30 years. Unlike seasonal flu that can cause anywhere from 1,000 to 50,000 annual deaths, a pandemic flu can cause hundreds of thousands to millions of deaths.

What is the "H" and the "N"?

In this book and in countless articles about pandemics, there are references to the types of influenza viruses noted as H1N1, H5N1, etc. What does the "H" mean and what does the "N" mean?

According to the CDC, the H stands for hemagglutinin and the N stand for neuraminidases. They are both types of proteins that are found on the outer shell of the virus.

The hemagglutinin is the protein that the virus uses to attach to the host cells. The neuraminidase is the protein that the virus uses to be released from the host cell so that it can use the M2 Ion Channel to move through the viral envelope to aid the virus' replication process.

How Does an Influenza Virus Mutate?

There are frequent references to influenza viruses that mutate from one form into another form that is more dangerous. It is important to have a basic understanding of how that happens because it explains why the flu vaccine has to change each year.

The Morgridge Institute for Research provides an excellent explanation of the process:

> *Influenza viruses can change in two different ways: antigenic drift and antigenic shift. Antigenic drift occurs more commonly and refers to small, gradual*

changes that occur through mutations in the genetic material that cause small changes in the surface proteins hemagglutinin and neuraminidase. Antigenic drift produces new virus strains that may not be recognized by the immune system, even if it has been primed (by vaccination or prior infection) to recognize other influenza strains. A person infected with a particular influenza strain creates antibodies that recognize that strain of the virus, but, if a new strain appears, the older antibodies will not recognize it, causing the person to become sick again. This is one reason a person may get the flu more than once during the flu season and why it is important to create vaccines against the viruses that are currently circulating the population. Every year the vaccine is updated to keep up with changes in the circulating influenza viruses so it is important to be immunized annually.

Disclaimer

This book is for general informational purposes only and should not be construed as advice concerning any specific set of public health circumstances or responses. The information, samples, templates, tips and techniques provided in this book are intended solely as examples of practices.

Purpose

Pandemic Influenza Planning: Information for Schools and Centers was designed as a working document that will need to be updated as circumstances and public health lessons are learned. The use of the book should be based on its relevancy to the school or center and should not be used if information about certain pandemics or epidemics is updated or revised. Typically, the possible usefulness of a book of this type is for no more than two to three years or until significant changes are discovered in viruses, the treatment of viruses, or the response to widespread virus infections.

This book includes pandemic operational actions "Levels" that are paired with the United States Government's pandemic "Intervals" system, which are both overlaid by the World Health Organization's pandemic "Phases." The levels serve as an example to schools and centers to guide the development of responses and actions based on the identification and evolution of a pandemic event. This system of levels, intervals and phases should help schools and centers as well as school districts to specify timely operational responses and decisions.

This book also includes an example of a Decision-Making Matrix that helps delineate areas of decision-making responsibilities during a pandemic event, so schools and centers can focus on local operational planning.

The decision whether or not to close schools rests with the leadership of the school, center, or school district, based on public health information and guidance, unless there is a state-declared emergency where in some states the governor has statutory authority to close schools.

It becomes an awkward situation for schools and centers when there is a pandemic and the national-level recommendation from public health officials is to close schools. What if the conditions necessary to justify the closure of schools and thereafter causing the disruption of families and businesses are not present at a local school or center? Then the school leadership has to make a decision whether to follow the recommendations from a national public health source or ignore the recommendations and risk a student or staff members becoming ill.

During a pandemic, schools and centers should rely heavily on the assistance of local community responders and agencies, particularly local boards of health. Relationships with these groups need to be established and cultivated long before a pandemic occurs. Working with local agencies before a pandemic event is present will decrease fear, anxiety, and confusion and will improve the response to a pandemic.

The theme of cooperation and interdependence between and among schools, centers, public health, and emergency responders is prevalent throughout this book. School districts are encouraged to collaborate with their local emergency management coordinators, their local public health officials, and other community stakeholders

Planning for Schools and Centers

to create a plan to assure a comprehensive and effective response to a pandemic.

This book includes information about on-line training sessions from the Federal Emergency Management Agency called the National Incident Management System (NIMS). NIMS developed on-line training sessions for school administrators and other school staff, as well sessions on basic Incident Command Center operations. The framework of any emergency plan, including pandemic influenza planning, should include the operational principles detailed in the NIMS training sessions. This book also includes many reference materials that are available from the Centers for Disease Control (CDC), as well as references and scientific references.

Detailed information, suggestions, and examples for local pandemic plan development are also provided in this book. *It should be noted that while these guidelines focus on a pandemic, many of the prevention and operational plans could be applied to an epidemic event.*

This book also includes specific considerations, examples, and samples to consider when developing a pandemic plan, such as:

1. prevention
2. education
3. operations
4. access control
5. surveillance
6. screening
7. infection precautions

8. infection control
9. communication methods for staff, parents, and community
10. school activities and operations;
11. local, state, and national responsibilities
12. recovery
13. resources

CHAPTER ONE

Background and History of Pandemics

Influenza, commonly called "the flu," is caused by the influenza virus, which infects the respiratory tract (nose, throat, lungs). Influenza usually spreads from person to person when an infected person coughs, sneezes, or talks, and the virus is sent into the air. Influenza can cause illness in all ages, and it is more likely than other viral respiratory infections, such as the common cold, to cause severe illness and life-threatening complications. Annually, more than 200,000 people in the United States are hospitalized with influenza-like symptoms. Should an influenza pandemic occur, the incidence of illness and death from influenza will likely dramatically increase worldwide.

Public Health authorities have identified characteristics and challenges unique to a pandemic such as:

1. When the pandemic influenza virus emerges, its global spread is considered inevitable.
2. Most people will have little or no immunity to a pandemic flu virus, and a significant percentage of the population could require medical care.
3. Death rates could be unpredictable due to the significant number of people who become infected, the virulence of the virus, and the characteristics and vulnerability of affected populations (elderly, those with chronic disease, and children).

Planning for Schools and Centers

4. Past pandemics have spread globally in two, and sometimes three, waves.
5. Medical supplies may be inadequate. Vaccine for the virus may not be available for months.
6. Hospital beds and other supplies may be limited.
7. Pandemics may also cause economic and social disruption such as schools and businesses closing, travel bans, and cancellation of community events.
8. Care of sick family members and fear of exposure can result in significant absenteeism in the workforce.

The first recorded influenza pandemic was in 1510 when an influenza virus spread throughout Africa and Europe. Epidemiological historians believe other influenza pandemics occurred between the 16th century and the 19th century. The details of the virus are unclear. We do know, however, that the number of deaths reached epic proportions and completely wiped out entire villages and towns and decimated cities.

The first pandemic that includes details and impact information was the "Asiatic Flu" first reported in May of 1889 in Russia. The 1889 influenza pandemic was not only the first pandemic in the modern era but also one of the first that was covered by the print news media in daily dispatches about the spread of the virus. Newspapers published in many European cities reported the spread of the disease in an up-to-date way and in an almost personal manner. The descriptions of the symptoms were in lurid details, and the specificity of the spread of the disease enabled readers and later scientists to understand how and where it spread.

The 1889 pandemic spread rapidly west and reached North America in December of 1889. In 1890, it spread to South America, India, and Australia. The influenza pandemic was caused by the H2N8 type of flu virus and had a very high attack and mortality rate. The global spread was aided by merchant ships that moved from port to port and the rapid expansion of railroads across Europe and into Russia. It is estimated that the virus killed over one million people worldwide.

The notorious pandemic of 1918, called the "Spanish Flu," lasted from 1918-1919. The influenza virus was first identified in March of 1918 in the United States at a military facility, Camp Funston, in Kansas, at the same time, it was reported in Europe and Asia. The spread of the virus was incredibly fast and it was deadly. It became the deadliest pandemic in modern history. By October of 1918, it had become a worldwide pandemic. In just six months, 25 million people died worldwide. An estimated 500,000 died in the United States. Many victims were young and otherwise healthy adults. It was common for a person to get sick and die the same day. In a desperate attempt to control the spread of the virus, citizens were ordered to wear masks. Schools, theaters, libraries, and other public places were ordered to close. Researchers later discovered what made the 1918 pandemic so deadly was because it invaded people's lungs and caused rapidly developed and deadly pneumonia.

The 1957 Asian flu originated in China and due to ships, railroads, and some airplanes, it spread rapidly across the globe. It lasted until late 1958. The 1957 pandemic caused an estimated 70,000 deaths in the United States where it attacked primarily people over the age of 55, young children, and pregnant women. The estimated worldwide death toll was between 1.5 million to 4 million. First identified in China in late February 1957, the virus spread to the United States by June. It was later determined that the virus was the H2N2. The very rapid development of a vaccine against the H2N2 virus and the availability of antibiotics to treat secondary lung infections limited the spread and mortality of the pandemic.

The Hong Kong Flu, 1968-1969, was an Influenza A virus that caused about 35,000 deaths in the United States and 700,000 worldwide. The new virus was first detected in Hong Kong in January of 1968 and reached the United States by June of that year with just a few cases. However, by September the virus was spreading into sections of the United States and became widespread by December 1968. Deaths from this virus peaked in December 1968 and January 1969. People over the age of 65 were most likely to die from the virus. Other age groups contracted the virus but typically they recovered. The number of deaths between September 1968 and March 1969 was 33,800, making it the mildest flu pandemic in the 20th century. The same virus, however, returned to the

United States and other parts of the world in 1970 and 1972, but not worldwide, with the same mortality rate as seasonal flu. It is speculated that the 1968 virus was similar to the 1957 virus so several people had an immunity to the virus. Furthermore, the peak of the 1968 virus hit while schools across the United States were on winter vacation or Christmas break from schools, which reduced the spread.

The 2009 H1N1 (Swine Flu) outbreak is an example of how quickly a flu virus can spread between and among people. The 2009 pandemic also revealed flaws in pandemic plans around the world but especially in the United States. The United States pandemic plan had a false assumption that any pandemic type of virus would originate overseas and thus there would be time for lab results and impact studies to determine the virility of the virus which would allow the United States time to determine its response. All of those plans were eviscerated when the genesis of the 2009 influenza virus was in Mexico and quickly spread to the United States, catching public health officials completely by surprise. In an attempt to control the spread of the virus, CDC issued school closure requirements that were quickly rescinded when it was determined that closing school was a very complicated event that could have a negative impact on the medical and health community workforce without significantly reducing the social contact that causes viruses to spread. Another surprise was the timing of the peak time of the virus, which typically is during the winter months. In the spring of 2009, a new flu virus spread quickly across the United States and the world. The first H1N1 (Swine Flu) case was diagnosed on April 15, 2009. By April 21, 2009, the CDC was working to develop a vaccine for the virus. On April 26, the United States government declared H1N1 a public health emergency and there were indications that the virus was spreading rapidly around the world. By June 30, 2009, over 75 countries reported several confirmed cases of H1N1. In July of that year, 18,000 cases of H1N1 had been reported in the United States. By November 2009, 48 states had reported cases of H1N1, mostly in young people. For various reasons, H1N1 vaccine supply was limited in the beginning, but over 61 million vaccine doses were ready by November. Reports of flu activity began to decline in parts of the country, which gave the United States a chance to vaccinate more than 80 million people against H1N1. CDC claimed that the vaccinations minimized the impact of the virus, but there is ample evidence that by then the virus had run its course and the vaccinations were primarily effective in preventing a return of the virus.

The CDC estimates that 43 million to 89 million people had H1N1 between April 2009 and April 2010. It is estimated that between 8,870 and 18,300 died from H1N1 related illness.

Current and Future Concerns About Influenza

The primary concern from scientists includes the Avian Flu (H5N1), also called the Bird Flu and/or another novel (new) virus that could develop, such as a mutated version of the Swine Flu (H1NI). The Avian Flu has a high mortality rate but seems to spread very slowly and has not become easily transferable from animal to man. The Swine Flu is not as deadly as the Avian Flu, but it spreads quickly and transfers easily from person to person.

The Avian Flu affects only birds or animals at first, but gradually changes to affect humans as well in some cases. Health officials have confirmed this virus subtype and the fact that humans do not have immunities to it. Additionally, there are cases where humans have become infected with the virus and have become severely ill. In fact, the mortality rate and pace of death are very high and fast.

A cross-virus that could develop from a virus such as Swine Flu commingling with another type of virus could spread more quickly than the Avian Flu because it transfers from human to human easily, just as easily as seasonal flu. This type of virus may not have a high mortality rate, but the outbreak spread could quickly infect large numbers of citizens. If this type of flu evolves, the rapidity of the event may dictate a quick response from public health officials which may include requiring school districts to implement social distancing and other measures.

Will There Be Another Pandemic

In a study of the possibility of another pandemic, hundreds of epidemiologists were surveyed. Over 90% of them said they thought there would be a pandemic within the next 10 to 20 years. Most of them indicated that the virility of the virus would be greater with estimates that 1 billion people would get sick; 165 million would die; there would be a global recession and depression; and there would be $1-3 trillion cost to the economies of the world. These dire predictions are for four primary reasons:

1. There is growing evidence that influenza viruses are continuing to mutate into more powerful forms, making the likelihood that a deadly virus will cross-match with a rapidly spreading virus to create a dangerous combined virus that can spread easily from person to person.
2. Dramatic increase in our global population size which means there are more people that will be infected and more people to spread the virus
3. More people are moving to central locations, clustering around cities and suburban centers. The closer proximity increases the risk of spreading viruses to more people at a faster rate.
4. More people are traveling within countries and around the world. World travel is at record levels and is increasing every year. More people than ever are traveling by airplane. A person who

becomes infected with a virus could conceivably in one day travel by airplane to another part of the word or to several countries within a hemisphere.

A scenario written by Robin Carlyle illustrates the point:

Let's say someone is infected with a novel strain of the flu, one that is spread from human-to-human-to-human. It's not a strain included in the flu vaccine, and antivirals aren't very effective at treating it. The first case pops up in -- say -- a farmer in northern India. That farmer goes to sell goods in New Delhi and comes into contact with another young man. The young man (now infected but not yet showing symptoms) flies out two days later to visit family in England and sits in the middle seat on a tightly-packed airplane. He's very chatty and talks the entire duration of the flight, sharing his respiratory droplets (and consequently the influenza virus) with his seat mates as well as the flight attendant. Upon arriving, the young man goes into the crowded streets of London to visit his family, while his new friends and the flight attendant continue on to their next flights to New York, Rio de Janeiro, and Paris, bringing the virus with them ... Within three weeks, the virus is spreading exponentially on 5 different continents, and health officials are only beginning to notice. (Carlyle, 2012)

Pandemic Impact at the State Level

The United States Department of Health and Human Services (HHS) has provided a state-by-state estimate of the impact of a pandemic. These estimates are divided into two categories: A "Moderate Outbreak" (1958 or 1968-like) and a "Severe Outbreak" (1918-like). In the Moderate Outbreak scenario in a state, for example, with 10 million citizens, approximately 2.2 million would become ill. Over 450,000 would require outpatient treatment and over 24,500 would need hospitalization. An estimated 6,100 would die from a Moderate impact virus.

In a Severe Outbreak scenario, approximately 2.2 million would become ill and over 450,000 citizens would require outpatient treatment. However, almost 60,000 would need hospital treatment and over 14,000 deaths would occur from a Severe Outbreak impact virus. Most states would not have enough hospital beds to meet the needs during a Severe Outbreak.

Even with a Moderate Outbreak, health care systems would be strained, as would other essential services. The availability of health care and education staff may be diminished which more heavily burdens the infrastructure of services. Due to the increase in the severity of the outbreak, the workforce of businesses most likely will decline which may lead to business closures during a Moderate Outbreak. This series of closures may limit public access to products and services. A Severe Outbreak would most likely require widespread, if not complete, school closures and would impact almost every segment of society, including access to schools, healthcare, services, products, and other sources of individual and family supports.

It should be noted that the 1918 flu outbreak impacted almost every town, city, and community in most states, even the most remote small towns, and communities. With modern transportation capability and mobility of citizens, a present day outbreak could spread more completely and rapidly than the 1918 outbreak.

CHAPTER TWO

Pandemic Planning and Training

When planning for a pandemic, the first step is to evaluate the current emergency management crisis plan (*see the Appendix for specific guidelines on developing crisis management plans*) and to ensure that an emergency planning team is in place to develop a pandemic plan. A checklist from the Centers for Disease Control and Prevention (CDC) is included in the Appendix. The CDC's Pandemic Influenza Planning Checklist provides a framework to begin an internal assessment.

1. Identify members of the emergency planning team, including, but not limited to: community stakeholders, local businesses, local emergency response agencies, public health, mental health, faith-based organizations, parents, school administration, school nurse, school psychologist, school counselor, teachers, students, information and communication technology, food services, transportation, and environmental services.

2. Appoint a pandemic influenza plan coordinator and co-coordinator.

3. Review and update school and center pandemic plan.

Planning for Schools and Centers

4. Partner closely with the local public health director to establish communication procedures for surveillance of disease and sharing of information before, during, and after an event.

5. Establish a chain of command and alternates, to include: an appropriate organization chart for the school, center, and the school district, clearly defined responsibilities, and communication networks and methods.

Pandemic Preparedness and Response Training

If pandemic planning team members need training in incident management and planning, the Federal Emergency Management Agency's Federal Management Institute offers National Incident Management System (NIMS) on-line training.

Several modules are available on-line, but the following provide the basic understanding of planning, incident command and communications.

Federal Emergency Management Agency Training (FEMA)

IS-100: Introduction to Incident Command System, I-100

As an introduction to the Incident Command System (ICS), this series provides the foundation for ICS training and includes a school staff training course. This course describes the history, features and principles, and organizational structure of the Incident Command System. It also explains the relationship between ICS and the National Incident Management System (NIMS).

IS-242: Effective Communication

The ability to communicate effectively is a vital part of every emergency manager, planner, and responder's job. This course is designed to improve your communication skills. It addresses:

1. Basic communication skills
2. How to communicate in an emergency
3. How to identify community communication issues
4. How to use technology as a communication tool
5. Effective oral communication
6. How to prepare an oral presentation

IS-362: Multi-hazard Emergency Planning for Schools

This course describes emergency management operations, roles, and duties; explains how to assess potential hazards that schools may face, and explains how to develop and test an Emergency Operations Plan that addresses all potential hazards. The course is designed for school administrators, principals, and first responders.

IS-700: National Incident Management System (NIMS), an Introduction

In 2003, Homeland Security developed the National Incident Management System (NIMS). The NIMS provides a consistent nationwide template to enable all government, private-sector, and nongovernmental organizations to interact during domestic incidents. This course explains the purpose, principles, key components, and benefits of NIMS.

Points to Consider During Planning

When planning for a pandemic or epidemic event,
leadership should consider the following:

Impact and Issues
1. Potential for school closings: full school closure
   or partial school closure where some schools are
   closed while others remain open
2. Large numbers of staff absent, difficult to
   maintain school operations
3. Loss of services from suppliers (e.g. food
   services and transportation)
4. Student absenteeism elevated above normal
   trends
5. Parents who choose to keep healthy children at
   home

Community Considerations
1. Large percentages of the population may be
   unable to work for days to weeks during a
   pandemic.
2. Significant numbers of people and expertise
   would be unavailable.
3. Emergency and essential services such as fire,
   police, and medical could be diminished.
4. School operations could be affected.
5. Methods of continued instruction should several
   schools close.

Planning for Schools and Centers

Basic Goals in Pandemic Planning

1. Limit illness, the spread of illness, and emotional trauma.
2. Preserve the continuity of essential functions.
3. Minimize social and educational disruption.
4. Minimize instructional loss.

Key Components to Pandemic Planning

1. Education and Prevention
   - ✓ Educating staff, students, and parents about good hygiene practices is a significantly important component of illness prevention and control.

2. Incident Command System
   - ✓ Establishing an Incident Command System will be essential for managing any type of emergency or event like a pandemic.

3. Communication
   - ✓ Establishing communication protocols and links is essential before an emergency like a pandemic emerges.
   - ✓ The communication protocol should include internal and external emergency contact lists and methods.

✓ The communication lists should be updated and verified on a regular basis.

4. Stakeholder Coordination
   ✓ The pandemic planning team should meet with, plan with, and work with local public health officials before and after a pandemic.

5. Surveillance (student and staff attendance)
   ✓ The school and local public health department should work together to establish a "sentinel" program to monitor student and staff attendance. For example, when student attendance drops below 80 percent, the school could send a notice to the local public health department. Student and staff absences may be an early indicator of a widespread virus event.

6. Prepare for Partial or Full Closing of Schools or School District
   ✓ Consider various models and possibilities related to school and staff assignments.
   ✓ Review bus routes and broaden alternative bus routes and create a

contingency plan if there is a shortage of bus drivers.

✓ Work on plans with local agencies to assist families.

✓ Develop a plan to monitor the conditions of school employees to determine if there will be a teacher and critical area shortages, such as food services employees, bus drivers, and administrators.

7. Alternatives to Closing Schools
    ✓ Implement social distancing.
    ✓ Eliminate field trips.
    ✓ Reduce or postpone extracurricular activities.
    ✓ Set "screeners" at school entrance to screen out students and staff with flu-like symptoms to prevent them from going to classes.

8. Educational Continuity
    ✓ In the event that schools have to close, what strategies will be in place to continue education in some form? How will school work continue for students whose school is closed while other schools remain open in the same school district? This difficult task should be part

Planning for Schools and Centers

of the pandemic planning team's discussions and plans.

✓ Consider the use of computers, internet access, and other electronic and technical mean to provide some type of instruction should schools close for a prolonged period of time.

9. Recovery

✓ Each pandemic plan should address the complexities of recovery.

✓ Reopening schools that have been closed for a prolonged period of time is a complicated task that includes inspecting the school building; determining how many staff members are well enough to return to work; reestablishing service schedules with vendors (e.g., food deliveries), and much more.

✓ This book provides an example of Recovery Phases, including recovery of essential services, staffing, and health concerns prior to reopening schools.

Pandemic Planning Team Responsibilities and Considerations

1. Develop the preparedness and pandemic response plan using levels; include Decision Forms to create a decision archive for the event (decision archives are essential for debriefings, for justification of decisions, and for possible federal and state reimbursements).
2. Identify school staff members responsible for activating the pandemic influenza plan (it is advisable to have backup staff members to fill in for absent staff members).
3. Consider and provide sufficient and accessible infection prevention supplies (contact the local public health department to determine what supplies are needed, such as N-95 masks, and to help with ordering the supplies).
4. Consider provision of sufficient school operation supplies (food, cleaning supplies, paper supplies) during a pandemic when schools are open.
5. Develop a process with the local public health department to report a substantial increase in absenteeism among students and faculty.
6. Identify methods to reduce the spread of the virus.
7. Plan for the identification and screening of students and staff with flu-like symptoms.

8. Plan for the care of students who are ill and determine when ill students may return to school.
9. Determine how ill students at the school will be isolated until parents arrive.
10. Plan for continuity of operations and identify essential services.
11. Communicate the plan to division administrative staff, school staff, parents/guardians, students, parents, and the community.
12. Provide information to families for the development of individual family plans (advise them to refer to the CDC website for families).
13. Plan for the delivery of educational services in the event that a significant number of staff members become ill but the school remains open.
14. Plan for the orderly closure or partial closure of school operations, ongoing instruction, and eventual school reopening.
15. Coordinate school closure or partial closure with neighboring school districts.
16. Discuss the needs of international students, disabled students, and impoverished students.
17. Plan for the use of school facilities by community partners during a pandemic if the schools are closed or partially closed (i.e., vaccinations).

Planning for Schools and Centers

18. Develop contingency plans for student annual assessments. Work with the state department of education on the state accountability assessments.
19. Review the pandemic plan and update as necessary, based on conditions, circumstances, new information, and new guidance from public health.
20. Participate in any and all pandemic table-top exercises conducted by local or state public health and/or the local or state office of emergency planning.

Pandemic Outbreak Response Suggestions and Sample Planning Components

Information regarding the occurrence of a pandemic in a community is typically provided by the state and local health departments and others designated by the State or Federal officials.

State and Federal responses to a pandemic will be guided by the World Health Organization (WHO), United States Department of Health and Human Services, CDC, and the recommendations of each State Division of Public Health.

The following sample planning components are based on operational actions translated from WHO and CDC. The levels include specific considerations during each event level of the pandemic and are matched with United States Government (USG) Intervals. Local school districts, based on their local pandemic plan and assistance and guidance from local public health, can take action at each event level – ranging from prevention, a high state of alertness, action, and then recovery.

The following provides suggestions and examples for activities and operational plans in response to the spread of a pandemic. It is not intended to cover or include all activities, strategies, possibilities or contingencies.

It should be noted that it is possible a pandemic would spread rapidly within a few days, so schools may have to close at some time during Levels 3-6. It is also possible that some schools will close when others remain open.

CHAPTER THREE

Primary Pandemic Preparation and Response

This chapter details specific responses to various severity levels of a pandemic. As the circumstances and mortality rate of the pandemic virus become known, stages of response protocols should be reviewed and activated upon verification of information.

The following levels of response are examples of what should be considered when activating a pandemic response plan. Since schools and centers will receive information about a pandemic from the World Health Organization (WHO), CDC (referred to as United States Government or USG), and from state and local sources, it is important to understand the terminology and the intent of the different response levels.

The WHO developed six "phases" to describe the development and spread of a pandemic: Interim phases 1 and 2; Pandemic Alert Period phases 3-5; and Pandemic Period phase 6. USG developed more descriptive and definable "stages, but after the H1N1 event in 2009 CDC changed to "Intervals, as noted below.

United States Government Pandemic Intervals

Investigation Interval: Investigation of Novel Influenza Cases

The investigation interval is initiated by the identification and investigation of a novel influenza An infection in humans or animals anywhere in the world that is judged by subject-matter experts to have potential implications for human health.

Public health actions focus on targeted surveillance and epidemiologic investigations to identify human infections and assess the potential for the virus to cause severe disease in humans, including person-to-person transmission, co-investigations of animal outbreaks with animal health representatives, and consideration of case-based control measures (i.e., antiviral treatment and antiviral post-exposure prophylaxis of contacts for infected humans and isolation of humans and animals who are infected).

After recognition of a case of novel influenza infection in a human, as occurred with the H7N9 and H3N2v viruses, animal investigations subsequently identified circulation of influenza viruses in birds and swine, respectively, and identified the reservoir of the previously unrecognized novel influenza viruses. CDC conducts an assessment during the investigation interval to characterize the potential for emergence, and if the virus does emerge, the severity of the human infection. Generally, identification of human cases of novel influenza

An infection is reported to WHO in accordance with the International Health Regulations.

Recognition Interval:
Recognition of Increased Potential for Ongoing Transmission

The recognition interval is initiated when increasing numbers of human cases or clusters of novel influenza An infection are identified anywhere in the world, and the virus characteristics indicate an increased potential for ongoing human-to-human transmission.

Public health actions concentrate on control of the outbreak, with a focus on the potential use of case-based control measures, including treatment and isolation of ill persons and voluntary quarantine of contacts.

Initiation Interval: Initiation of the Pandemic Wave

The initiation interval begins when human cases of a pandemic influenza virus infection are confirmed anywhere in the world with demonstrated efficient and sustained human-to-human transmission.

The definition of efficient and sustained transmission is established during an event based on the epidemiologic characteristics of the emerging virus. For example, efficient transmission could be defined as a household or an institutional attack rate of $\geq 20\%$ in more than two communities, and sustained could be defined as the transmission of virus for three or more generations in more than one cluster.

Planning for Schools and Centers

Continued implementation of case-based control measures and routine personal protective measures (e.g., hand hygiene) is essential, as is enhanced surveillance for detecting additional cases of the novel virus to determine when community mitigation measures will be implemented. If possible, tests results should be used to ensure that actions are proportional to the severity of the disease caused by the virus.

Acceleration Interval: Acceleration of the Pandemic Wave

The acceleration interval is indicated by a consistently increasing rate of pandemic influenza cases identified in the United States, indicating established transmission. Consideration of immediate initiation of appropriate community mitigation measures such as school and child-care facility closures and social distancing in addition to the efficient management of public health resources (including medical countermeasures and vaccines, if available) are of primary importance in this interval and are guided by tests results. Isolation and treatment of ill persons and voluntary quarantine of contacts continue as key mitigation measures.

Historical analyses and mathematical modeling indicate that early institution of combined, concurrent community mitigation measures might maximize the reduction of disease transmission and subsequent mortality in the affected areas.

Planning for Schools and Centers

Deceleration Interval: Deceleration of the Pandemic Wave

The deceleration interval is indicated by a consistently decreasing rate of pandemic influenza cases in the United States. During this interval, planning for appropriate suspension of community mitigation measures and recovery begins. State or local health officials might rescind community mitigation measures in certain regions within their jurisdiction when no new cases are occurring or are occurring infrequently.

Preparation Interval: Preparation for a Subsequent Pandemic Wave

The preparation interval is characterized by low pandemic influenza activity, although outbreaks might continue to occur in certain jurisdictions. Primary actions focus on discontinuing community mitigation measures; facilitating the recovery of the public health, health-care, and community infrastructure; resuming enhanced surveillance protocols to detect subsequent waves; evaluating the response to the initial wave, and preparing for potential additional waves of infection. Because this interval can last from weeks to months, planning and preparation for a subsequent pandemic wave should reflect this variability.

A pandemic is declared ended when evidence indicates that influenza, worldwide, is transitioning to seasonal patterns of transmission.

Like the 2009 H1N1 strain, pandemic strains might circulate for years after the pandemic, gradually taking on the behavior and transmission patterns of seasonal influenza viruses.

Applying WHO and USG Pandemic Phases and Intervals to Operations

The WHO phases and the USG intervals do not together offer sufficient overlap and matching to be useful to schools and centers. However, they will be the official notification mechanism and can and should be used to guide operation decisions.

In this chapter, to aid schools and centers a practical interpretation of the WHO and USG pandemic intervals is offered that provides some examples of operational responses to a pandemic. They are not all-inclusive and are based on how decisions have to be made for schools to operate.

World Health Organization
(attached to the United Nations)
World Health Organization
(WHO)
United States Government represents the Centers for Disease Control, Homeland Security, National Guard, and Emergency Management
United States Government
(USG)
Public Education
(PE)
Pandemic Event Designations
- *WHO Phase I* and *WHO Phase II* are equivalent to *USG Interval Investigation* and *PE Level 0*

- *WHO Phase 3* is equivalent to *USG Interval Recognition* and *PE Level 1*
- *WHO Phase 4* and *WHO Phase 5* are equivalent to *USG Interval Initiation and Acceleration* and *PE Levels 2, 3,* and *4*
- *WHO Phase 6 – Pandemic Period* is equivalent to *USG Declaration and Recovery* and *PE Levels 5 and 6*

The WHO does not designate a Pandemic Recovery Period or a Pandemic Event End Period, but Recovery is *USG Interval Preparation* and *PE Level 7*

NOTE: Depending on circumstances, it may be necessary to either move rapidly from one level to another or skip levels in order to respond to event circumstances. These are examples and are intended to serve only as reminders of essential functions and considerations.

Level 0: Prevention and Preparations

- ✓ Place posters on hand washing and infection control in schools and on the website.
- ✓ Provide information to schools, parents, and staff about hand sanitizers, cough and sneeze etiquette, signs and symptoms of influenza.
- ✓ Ensure custodial staff has appropriate training on proper cleaning and disinfecting work and play areas.
- ✓ Ensure schools and departments have adequate supplies (soaps, hand sanitizers, etc.).
- ✓ Check First Aid Kits and add N95 face masks for school nurses and other staff.
- ✓ Establish and test emergency communication protocol with staff contact "tree."
- ✓ Provide information to staff and parents on pandemic planning for families.
- ✓ Develop Incident Command Center protocol, location, equipment and assign staff.
- ✓ Develop plans for operating with staff workforce reduction.
- ✓ Develop plans to secure buildings, information technology, and finance.
- ✓ Encourage employees to use Direct Deposit.
- ✓ Encourage parents to have alternative child care plans.

  Develop alternatives to closing schools (i.e., implement social distancing; eliminate field trips; reduce or postpone extracurricular

Planning for Schools and Centers

activities; set "screeners" at school entrance to screen out students and staff with flu-like symptoms to prevent them from going to classes.)

✓ Develop plans for educational continuity if schools close:

- Study packets and suggested activities for students and parents
- Web-based education (i.e., on-line classes; virtual school; education blogs; home school educational websites)

✓ Find out if vendors in the supply chain have a pandemic or emergency plan for continuity or recovery of supply deliveries.

✓ Plan for full school district closure and partial school closure (i.e., some schools closed while others remain open within the same school district).

✓ Develop a mental health plan for students and staff, in conjunction with local mental health services staff to implement during a pandemic event and during the recovery phase; the plan should include Post-Traumatic Stress Syndrome counseling.

✓ Develop Human Resources employee emergency contact lists and reciprocal contact procedures; Human Resources should conduct a study of critical infrastructure staff with young

Planning for Schools and Centers

children (because they are more likely to remain home during a widespread illness event) to determine if redundancy plans are necessary; develop a Fitness for Duty checklist to determine if an employee is ready to return to work and under what conditions.

✓ Local school superintendent should establish a command structure in the event that he or she is unable to continue work during the pandemic event or is unable to return to work during the recovery phase; develop central office teleconferencing protocol in the event that schools are closed.

✓ Develop plans to conduct table-top exercises to practice and refine the pandemic plan.

✓ Apply all plans and procedures to after-school programs.

Level 1: Suspected Human-to-Human Outbreak

- ✓ Review pandemic plan for preparedness and provide ongoing communication to key staff on their roles and responsibilities.
- ✓ Maintain all infection control precautionary measures.
- ✓ Keep staff and parents current with updates through the school district website and cable access channel, if available; ask PTA or PTSA to assist with updated messages; make certain that health-related information and pandemic updates have been verified for accuracy by the local health department.
- ✓ Ensure all staff and external contact information is current, including direct lines to the local health department.
- ✓ Open the direct link to local health department.
- ✓ Alert all principals of Event Level 1 status and remind them that the Event Level may escalate rapidly to the next Level or Levels.
- ✓ Monitor student and staff attendance daily and report to the local health department any school where student and/or staff attendance drops below 90 percent.
- ✓ Review out-of-country field trips and plans for future out-of-country field trips. Cancel out-of-country field trips to countries with human-to-human outbreak; review out-of-state field trips

and inform schools and parents that all future field trips may be canceled.

✓ Do not enroll students from out-of-country or out-of-state without appropriate immunization records, based on immunization and other health guidelines provided by the local health department, the State Division of Public Health and/or the United States Department of Health and Human Services.

✓ Place Incident Command Center staff on standby; remind appropriate staff of Incident Command Center duties and responsibilities.

✓ Provide information to the local health department on medically fragile children that may need specialized care at school or at home during a pandemic event; share local health department contact information with the parents of medically fragile children and provide guidance on how and who to contact at the local health department if their medically fragile child or children are at home due to long-term public and school closure.

✓ Inform community agencies (i.e., Red Cross, Board of Health, Traveler's Aid, etc.) of families that may not have access to food on a regular basis (i.e., indigent and homeless), that may have a language barrier that would impede their efforts to seek basic essentials during an outbreak, or other families that would have limited resources during a long-term outbreak.

✓ Some students may need specialized care at school or at home during a pandemic event; share local health department contact information with the parents of medically fragile children and provide guidance on how and who to contact at the local health department if their medically fragile child or children are at home due to long-term public and school closure.

✓ Inform community agencies (i.e., Red Cross, Board of Health, Traveler's Aid, etc.) of families that may not have access to food on a regular basis (i.e., indigent and homeless), that may have a language barrier that would impede their efforts to seek basic essentials during an outbreak, or other families that would have limited resources during a long-term outbreak.

✓ Meet with all daycare providers that use school district facilities or who receive students after school via school district school buses to inform them of pandemic response procedures and keep them up-to-date on health information and operational procedures.

✓ Apply all procedures to after-school programs.

Level 2: Confirmed Human Outbreak

✓ Conduct meeting with Incident Command Center staff to pre-stage full activation of Center.

✓ Provide ongoing communication to key staff on their roles and responsibilities.

✓ Maintain infection control precautionary measures.

✓ Keep staff and parents current with updates through the school district website and cable access channel, if available; ask PTA or PTSA to assist with updated messages; make certain that health-related information and pandemic updates have been verified for accuracy by the local health department.

✓ Alert all principals of Event Level 2 status and remind them that the Event Level may escalate rapidly to the next Level or Levels.

✓ Monitor student and staff attendance daily and report to the local health department any school where student and/or staff attendance drops below 90 percent.

✓ Do not enroll any students without appropriate immunization records, based on immunization and other health guidelines provided by the local health department, the State Division of Public Health and/or the United States Department of Health and Human Services.

Planning for Schools and Centers

✓ Develop continuous direct link to local health department; make plans with the local health department to establish daily communications if a widespread outbreak occurs overseas.

✓ Continue surveillance of staff, students, school visitors, and other personnel to help the local health department to monitor influenza-like symptoms; it would be helpful to local health departments if these reports at this level could be provided on a daily basis.

✓ Activate procedures to isolate students and staff that present flu-like symptoms; encourage parents to keep their children at home if they have flu-like symptoms and to let the school know about their child's symptoms; encourage staff to remain at home if they have flu-like symptoms and to report these symptoms to the school.

✓ Keep relevant groups informed through cable access channel, e-mails, newsletters, fact sheets, and websites (i.e., booster clubs, activity clubs).

✓ Meet with hot-line information staff to review possible activation of the hotline information based on events occurring at this time.

✓ Remind staff, students, and parents of good hygiene practices.
✓ Consider canceling all out-of-country field trips or alert the chaperones.
✓ Review all out-of-state (in-country) field trips and be prepared to cancel all out-of-state field trips. Alert parents that future field trips may be canceled.
✓ Do not allow students or staff members into the school that presents influenza-like symptoms; monitor students and staff closely for flu-like symptoms.
✓ Prepare to implement educational continuity plans.
✓ Apply all procedures to after-school programs.

Level 3: Widespread Human Outbreak

- ✓ Activation of Incident Command Center and pre-stage 24/7 manning of Center; bring in extra phones (and cell phones) and computers; meet with Incident Command Center staff to prepare for a rapid escalation of the outbreak to North America; remind staff of roles and responsibilities and importance of access at any time.
- ✓ Activate daily direct link to the local health department and, if possible, to the State Emergency Operations Center and/or State Health Division via local agencies.
- ✓ Prepare information hotline for parents and staff; alert information hotline staff to report for a practice run of the hotline.
- ✓ Keep staff and parents current with updates through the school district website and cable access channel, if available; ask PTA or PTSA to assist with updated messages; make certain that health-related information and pandemic updates have been verified for accuracy by the local health department.
- ✓ Alert all principals of Event Level 3 status and remind them that the Event Level may escalate rapidly to the next Level or Levels.
- ✓ Monitor student and staff attendance daily and report to the local health department.

Planning for Schools and Centers

✓ Alert central office staff to the possible full school district or partial school closure.

✓ Alert central office staff to the possible cancellation of extracurricular activities.

✓ Continue surveillance of staff, students, school visitors, and other personnel to help the local health department to monitor influenza-like symptoms; it would be helpful to local health departments if these reports at this level could be provided on a daily basis.

✓ Cancel and call back all out-of-state field trips and ensure that all out-of-country field trips have been canceled and called back.

✓ Do not enroll new students without immunization records or approval from the local health department, based on immunization and other health guidelines provided by the local health department, the State Division of Public Health and/or the United States Department of Health and Human Services.

✓ Sanitize schools and buses daily, as per local health department guidelines; implement sanitizing verification process.

✓ Restrict school visitors to parents and vendors; be alert to parents or vendors with flu-like symptoms.

Planning for Schools and Centers

- ✓ Isolate ill students and staff in pre-determined locations in the school with supervision until they can be sent home or picked up by authorized persons.
- ✓ Pre-stage Crisis Management Team to discuss updated pandemic information and possible timeline for activation of the Team (or teams.)
- ✓ Pre-stage educational continuity plans.
- ✓ Apply all procedures to after-school programs; provide daily updated outbreak information to after-school programs and staff.

Level 4: Expanded Human Outbreak

- ✓ Full activation of Incident Command Center for all direct report staff, with a direct link to the local health department and, if possible, to the State Emergency Operations Center and/or State Health Division via local agencies.
- ✓ Alert Secondary Incident Command Center staff, in case primary staff members, are unable to man the Incident Command Center.
- ✓ Activate information hotline for parents and staff; update hotline information daily (at least), website information, and provide media updates (in collaboration with local health department and/or State Division of Public Health); make certain that health-related information and pandemic updates have been verified for accuracy by the local health department and/or State Division of Public Health.
- ✓ Activate Crisis Management Team for student and staff psychological support.
- ✓ Closely monitor staff and student attendance and provide reports to the local health department twice daily and to the Incident Command Center.
- ✓ Do not enroll new students without immunization records or approval from the

local health department, based on immunization and other health guidelines provided by the local health department, the State Division of Public Health and/or the United States Department of Health and Human Services.

✓ Human Resources reports to the Incident Command Center when any school, service, or support absences escalate.

✓ Human Resources contacts substitute or replacement teachers and other staff to determine availability for staffing.

✓ Pre-stage implementation of Educational Continuity Plans (i.e., study packets; cable access; local library system; on-line classes, etc.).

✓ Pre-stage alternatives to school closure:
- Gatherings of groups larger than normal class size may be limited during the school day (e.g. assemblies, recess).
- Prepare for possible cancellation of extracurricular activities.
- All field trips canceled or called back.
- Review extracurricular activities.
- Do not accept students or staff with flu-like symptoms.

- Student distance spacing strategies to decrease contact with students who may be infected but not exhibiting symptoms.
  - It is recommended that students' desks be spaced three (3) feet apart.
  - Discourage prolonged congregation in hallways and lunchrooms.
  - Limit group activities and interaction between classes.
  - Cancel or modify gym class, choir or other school activities that place individuals in close proximity.

✓ Pre-stage partial school closure or full school closure.

✓ Isolate and send home staff or students with flu-like symptoms.

✓ An appropriate room for isolation should have been designated and will be utilized and supervised at this time. Access to this room should be strictly limited and monitored.

✓ A school bus may be designated to transport sick students home (buses should be used in this capacity ONLY as an emergency measure when no one is available to pick the child up at school); buses should have an adult monitor.

- ✓ Students and staff with flu-like symptoms will be asked to stay home. Absences should be reported to the school attendance office throughout the school day, instead of once a day.
- ✓ Those allowed into the school building will be screened for flu-like symptoms. Each person cleared to enter the building will be given something to indicate that they are free to enter the building (e.g. a sticker, a card, a stamp on their hand).
- ✓ Adults and students accompanied by an adult may be excluded from entry into the school and instructed to call their health care providers for advice and evaluation.
- ✓ If a person warrants medical evaluation, health services staff should alert the local health department that a suspect case needs evaluation so that the health department can provide guidance.
- ✓ Alter school cleaning routines by maintenance staff.
  - o Disinfect work areas, counters, restrooms, doorknobs, and stair railings more frequently.

- o The school health office and holding areas for ill children should be cleaned at least twice each day and preferably throughout the day, in the morning before students arrive and in the afternoon after students leave the area.
- o Air conditioning system filters should be cleaned and changed frequently.
- o Telephones, pencils, pens, etc. should not be shared.
- o Specialized cleaning solutions are not essential. Standard cleaning products can disinfect surfaces (note: soap and water may not disinfect surfaces). The frequency of cleaning is most important.
- o During the day, where operationally possible, increase ventilation to the facility to decrease the spread of disease. Following each school day, the   school should be thoroughly ventilated and cleaned: opening all doors and windows or turning the air conditioning/heating systems up.
- ✓ Apply all procedures to after-school programs; provide daily updates.

Level 5: Expanded (local) Outbreak

- ✓ Full activation of Incident Command Center 24/7
- ✓ Maintain daily link to the local health department and, if possible, to the State Emergency Operations Center and/or State Health Division via local agencies.
- ✓ Prepare for communication links from public health and/or State Department of Education
- ✓ Human Resources reports to the Incident Command Center when any school, service, or support absences escalate.
- ✓ Partial school or full school closure or alternatives to closure, as recommended by public health.
- ✓ All field trips canceled or called back, including local field trips.
- ✓ Cancellation of extracurricular activities.
- ✓ Prepare Educational Continuity Plans (i.e., study packets; cable access; local library system; on-line classes, etc.) for rapid activation.
  - ▪ Pre-developed Study packets and suggested activities for students
  - ▪ Web-based education:
    - o On-line classes
    - o Virtual school
    - o Education Blogs

- o Homeschool educational websites
- ✓ Do not enroll any new students without immunization records or approval from the local health department, based on immunization and other health guidelines provided by the local health department, the Division of Public Health and/or the United States Department of Health and Human Services.
- ✓ Expand hotline staff and update hotline information, website information, and provide media updates; provide updates from the public health department, from the district superintendent, and, if necessary, from local law enforcement and public utilities and services; encourage parents to keep ill children at home and encourage ill staff to remain at home.
- ✓ Monitor students getting off buses and out of vehicles for signs of flu-like symptoms; do not accept students or staff with flu-like symptoms, **or** quickly isolate students and staff with flu-like symptoms.
- ✓ Isolate and send home staff or students with flu-like symptoms, utilizing supervised isolation areas in the school; access to this room should be strictly limited and monitored (i.e., parents picking up their ill

children should be escorted to and from the isolation area); a carefully monitored student checkout system should be activated.

✓ A school bus may be designated to transport sick students home; the school bus or buses should include adult monitors who may be asked to walk students to their homes from the bus (buses should be used in this capacity ONLY as an emergency measure when no one is available to pick the child up at school).

✓ Students and staff who have flu-like symptoms should be asked to stay home; add this information to the information hotline.

✓ Absences should be reported to the school attendance office throughout the day, with staffing absences reported to Human Resources as soon as possible, but at least twice daily.

✓ Access to the school building will be limited; persons presenting flu-like symptoms will not be allowed into the building; if a parent is at school to pick up his or her child before normal dismissal, the student will be brought to the parent outside the building; each person cleared to enter the building will be given something to indicate that they are free to enter the building (e.g. a sticker, a card, a stamp on their hand).

✓ If a person warrants medical evaluation, health services staff should alert the appropriate medical resources (i.e., public health) that a suspect case needs evaluation so that the referral center can make arrangements for a health assessment.

✓ Activate social distancing strategies:
   o Gatherings of groups larger than normal class size should be canceled and avoided (e.g. assemblies, recess).
   o Cancel all extra-curricular activities.
   o Student distance spacing strategies to decrease contact with students who may be infected but not exhibiting symptoms.
      ▪ Separate student desks as much as possible
      ▪ Prohibit congregation in hallways and lunchrooms; if possible, serve box lunches in classrooms to avoid gathering of students in the cafeteria; stagger class changes to avoid large groups of students in the hallway; stagger dismissal for the same reason; cancel gym

class, choir or other school activities that place individuals in close proximity.

- If possible stagger bus routes to reduce the number of students on each bus.

✓ Expand school cleaning routines by maintenance staff.

  o Disinfect all work areas, counters, restrooms, doorknobs, and stair railings several times daily; use other staff to assist, if necessary (specialized cleaning solutions are not essential; standard cleaning products can disinfect surfaces; the frequency of cleaning is most important).

  o The school health office and holding areas for ill children and staff should be cleaned several times each day.

  o Air conditioning system filters should be cleaned and changed frequently.

  o Telephones, pencils, pens, etc. should not be shared.

  o During the day, where operationally possible, increase ventilation to the facility to decrease the spread of disease. Following each school day, the   school should be thoroughly ventilated and cleaned: opening all doors and windows or turning the air conditioning/heating systems up.

✓ Apply all procedures to after-school programs; provide daily updated outbreak information to after-school programs and staff.

Level 6: Health Emergency

✓ Based on a directive from public health, the Governor or a joint decision between public health and the local school system, the superintendent orders a partial closure of schools. Depending on circumstances, it may be one or more schools.

OR

✓ Based on a directive from public health, the Governor or a joint decision between public health and the local school system, the superintendent closes all school building units and other department building units of the school district; the closure applies to all after-school programs and extracurricular activities. NOTE: It is possible that the first "order" or "recommendation" is to close only those schools with pandemic flu-related absences, so be prepared for partial school closures and preventing students from the affected school trying to enroll in other schools).

✓ Confirm closure with the State Department of Education.

✓ Inform the public and school district employees using all means of communication (i.e., press release; hotline recording; website emergency message; cable access; etc.); coordinate news release

Planning for Schools and Centers

with public health and the State Department of Education.

✓ Secure all buildings.

✓ School system police or other law enforcement agencies should check all buildings and establish periodic patrols during the school closure period.

✓ All perishable food items should be disposed of unless the cafeteria remains open.

✓ Check all alarm and surveillance systems.

✓ Secure information technology system and integrity.

✓ Secure all school buses and service vehicles.

✓ If possible, maintain Incident Command Center operations and essential services; if not possible, central office staff should maintain telephone contact on a regular basis with the superintendent, such as daily conference calls.

✓ Maintain communications with the local health department through the superintendent and/or designated staff.

✓ When possible, collaborate with local agencies to assist families.

✓ Activate Educational Continuity Plan
  o Distribute pre-developed study packets and suggested activities for students and parents
  o Web-based education possibilities:

Planning for Schools and Centers

- ✓ Cable Access educational television (with closed caption)
- ✓ Cable Educational shows (with closed caption)
- ✓ Video-streaming (with closed caption)
- ✓ Textbook and study guide depositories with drive-through capabilities
- ✓ Virtual classes on-line
- ✓ Teleconferencing

Levels 7: Recovery – Taking Steps to Reopen Schools and Centers

✓ Based on communication with public health and authorization to start the process of recovery, the school district will begin the initial stages of preparations for the re-opening of schools.

✓ Re-establish Incident Command Center as soon as possible.

✓ Human Resources will begin the process of compiling phone tree results indicating which staff members are ready to return to work, **OR** establish an Employee Hotline Phone Bank so employees can call in status (name; position; work location; health status; return to work date); use a pre-determined Fitness for Duty checklist to determine if an employee is ready to return to work and under what conditions.

✓ Human Resources will develop a status report for each staff category by school and department: teachers, administrators, bus drivers, custodians, etc.

✓ When possible, the Crisis Management Team staff will meet to activate the mental health plan for students and staff, in conjunction with local mental health services staff, including Post-Traumatic Stress Syndrome counseling.

✓ Inspect all buildings, facilities, equipment, materials, etc. and determine status and needs for operations. Maintain a status update for facilities not ready for occupancy.

✓ Inspect all buses.

✓ Survey supply vendors to determine when supply chain and delivery system will be partially or fully operational; provide vendors with supply needs.

✓ Finance department determines the process for fast-tracking purchase orders for essential supplies.

✓ Determine information technology status and operational needs; this will be related to financial technology, also.

✓ Inspect all school cafeterias with the assistance of the local health department.

✓ Expand all school cleaning routines by maintenance staff.

  o Disinfect all work areas, counters, restrooms, doorknobs, and stair railings several times daily; use other staff to assist, if necessary (specialized cleaning solutions are not essential; standard cleaning products can disinfect surfaces; the frequency of cleaning is most important).

  o Air conditioning system filters should be cleaned and changed.

- o The school should be thoroughly ventilated and cleaned: opening all doors and windows or turning the air conditioning/heating systems up.
- ✓ Establish a timeline and staffing threshold for opening schools and other buildings for staff, based on reports from Human Resources, building and bus inspections, and the local health department; determine which schools can open and if temporary consolidation of schools is appropriate. Include other agencies in the discussion about re-opening schools, such as DFACS, public health, mental health, fire marshal and fire department, public law enforcement, public transportation, etc.
- ✓ Share timeline for opening with news media and place recording on school district main phone line; also add to school district website.
- ✓ Some schools may remain closed until facility and/or staffing requirements are met.
- ✓ Re-activate information hotline as soon as possible.
- ✓ Post information on school district website for parents regarding helping children cope with tragedies (i.e., "Teaching Children How to Respond to Tragedies" from the National Association of School Psychologists).
- ✓ Provide parents with an updated school year calendar.

Planning for Schools and Centers

✓ Begin discussions on restructuring and resuming extra-curricular activities and after-school programs.

✓ The opening of schools should be monitored closely by Command Center staff.

✓ Daily reports of staff and student attendance should be closely monitored.

✓ A mental health status report, based on guidelines provided by the counselors and the Crisis Management Team, should be provided to the Command Center each day. This report should include the mental status of students and staff in order to determine if additional mental health services are needed.

✓ School nurses should compile daily health reports for the Command Center.

✓ Develop an "instructional reconstruction" checklist (base on the length of school closure; if short-term, the checklist should be focused on make-up school work and reorganizing the instructional calendar, benchmarks, testing, etc.; if the closure was long-term, the checklist may require restructuring of the current and the immediate following school year instructional and operational calendar and events) to guide staff, students, and parents when school reopens. The reconstruction checklist should include anticipated instructional materials and supplies, as well as possible waivers from the State Department of Education.

✓ Schools should not enroll new students without immunization records or approval from the local health department, based on immunization and other health guidelines provided by the local health department, the State Division of Public Health and/or the United States Department of Health and Human Services.

✓ Even when schools re-open, many students may need homebound instruction. A shortage of homebound teachers may be mitigated by maintaining the Educational Continuity Plan

  o Distribute pre-developed study packets and suggested activities for students and parents

  o Web-based education considerations:

    ▪ Cable Access educational television with closed caption

    ▪ Cable Educational shows with closed caption

    ▪ Video-streaming with closed caption, textbooks with accompanying study guide depositories and drive-through capabilities

    ▪ Teleconferencing

✓ When schools re-open activate social distancing strategies (to minimize possible infection spread):

✓ Gatherings of groups larger than normal class size should be canceled and avoided (e.g. assemblies, recess).

✓ Student distance spacing strategies to decrease contact with students who may be infected but not exhibiting symptoms.

- Separate student desks as much as possible
- Prohibit congregation in hallways and lunchrooms; if possible, serve box lunches in classrooms to avoid gathering of students in the cafeteria; stagger class changes to avoid large groups of students in the hallway; stagger dismissal for the same reason; cancel gym class, choir or other school activities that place individuals in close proximity.
- If possible, stagger bus routes so there are fewer students on each bus.

CHAPTER FOUR

Additional Planning Components and Details

It is important to consider necessary actions that are not obvious until situations arise. The following should be considered, depending on circumstances and the conditions and locations of the schools and centers.

Access Control

1. Develop a policy that enables school administrators to control access to the buildings.
2. Each school should have the plan to lock down certain entrances and exits and to monitor others, if necessary.
3. Identify the main entrance and an indoor screening area where students and staff will be screened prior to moving to classrooms or other areas of the building for each school.

Surveillance, Screening, and Triage

During all stages of a pandemic flu outbreak, it will be essential to monitor and document the number of students and faculty who are absent and meet the definition of influenza-like illness.

Keeping track of these numbers will help the school and health officials determine when and whether to close schools, whether the epidemic is increasing in scope and whether to declare an epidemic, making schools eligible to apply for reimbursement of ADA funds during increased absenteeism.

The following is an example:

1. Building-level school health services personnel (registered nurses, licensed practical nurses, nursing assistants, or principal's designee) will develop a plan to screen all students and staff. Younger children may be observed by health services personnel for a cough. Older children may be asked the following question: "Do you have a new cough that has developed over the last 10 days?"
2. School health services personnel will provide staff and students who have a cough with tissues. Surgical masks are not appropriate for all situations but are for specific health care situations.
3. School health services personnel will document screening data and review each week for analysis of trends.

Planning for Schools and Centers

4. The school nurse will evaluate individuals who have a new cough or fever (temperature ≥ 100.4) and place all individuals who have a fever and a new cough on droplet precautions, pending further evaluation.

5. Students who have been identified as ill will be placed in an identified isolation room for sick children until picked up by parents.

6. Local school district health services staff have the authority to restrict individuals (staff and students) who have a fever and a new cough from work, class, or any other group gathering. They also have the authority to send any student or staff home. Absenteeism will be monitored for any trends. School health staff will work with school administrators, social workers, and attendance clerks to monitor absentee trends. Significant trends will be reported to the School Nurse Coordinator or School Health Contract Person, who will inform the Superintendent and the local health department.

7. Infection control posters will be placed at all school entrances and commons areas.

8. Poster information will include health tips for protection against the spread of the flu and other germs and viruses.

9. The School Health Services Nurse Coordinator will monitor national, regional, and local data related to epidemic respiratory infections.

Planning for Schools and Centers

Infection Control/Precautions

Infection control and taking necessary precaution is also critical in pandemic planning. The following is an example:

1. All staff, students, and visitors will use droplet precautions (private room and surgical mask within 3 feet of ill person) for all contact with any individual who has a new cough and fever until a diagnosis of a non-contagious respiratory illness or an infection requiring a higher level of precautions is made.
2. If students, staff or visitors present with symptoms while at school, they should be provided a mask while awaiting transportation away from the facility.
3. School staff will ask persons who have a new cough to wear a surgical mask or use tissues to cover their mouth and nose when coughing, and to use proper hand hygiene during the time they need to be in the school building (Note: wearing a surgical mask is not a guarantee of protection in a general setting).
4. Wash hands thoroughly and often: use soap and water and wash for at least 20 seconds. Use alcohol-based hand sanitizers when hand washing is not possible. It is advised that all classrooms have alcohol-based hand sanitizers available for use by students and staff.

5. Schools will advise all persons, including staff, students, and visitors, who have fever and cough to defer attending or visiting the school until their illness has resolved.

6. If an isolation room is in use, a precaution sign will be placed on the door.

7. Schools will maintain adequate supplies of surgical masks, waterless hand rub, surface cleaners and disinfectants, and tissues throughout public areas, classrooms, and meeting rooms and in the school health offices. All surfaces will be cleaned and disinfected with an Environmental Protection Agency (EPA)-registered household disinfectant labeled for activity against bacteria and viruses, an EPA-registered hospital disinfectant, or EPA-registered chlorine bleach/hypochlorite solution. Labeled instructions should always be followed when using any of these disinfectants.

8.   Maintain appropriate inventories of supplies.

9. Protocols for waste disposal must be developed.

10. Schools will display hand-washing posters and "Cover Your Cough" posters in high-traffic areas

Communication/Education

Develop an effective and sustainable plan for communication and promotion of messages relating to epidemic respiratory infections to internal and external audiences. The following is an example:

1. Infection control measures will be reviewed with staff, annually, as well as strategies for communicating information to health services providers in the event of an epidemic respiratory infection.
2. Translation services for languages in the represented student population will be provided.
3. A variety of media may be used to communicate with the school community including newsletters, take-home flyers, messages on school menus, websites, school TV channels, county TV channels, and phone hotlines.

CHAPTER FIVE

Additional Preparedness Activities

Routine vaccination against seasonal influenza establishes good health practices and may boost the immune system during a pandemic flu outbreak. Also, the establishment of a vaccination protocol could be critical in the event of a pandemic because all of the elements would be in place for a widespread emergency vaccination activation.

1. Encourage influenza vaccination during the influenza season to reduce morbidity from seasonal influenza transmission in school staff.
2. All eligible staff may be offered the opportunity to receive influenza vaccine. Collaborate with local health departments for this service. School nurses in collaboration with local health departments can hold vaccination clinics on designated days.
3. Provide staff with information for local clinics providing the influenza vaccine.
4. Educational and promotional materials can be provided to school staff to promote availability and desirability of influenza vaccine for all ages.

Regulatory Authority Regarding Public Health Matters

Regulatory authority is the power that the legislature gives an agency to enforce statutes, to develop regulations that have the force of law, and to assist the public in complying with laws and regulations.

The power that can be delegated and the method of the delegation are determined by state constitutions and laws and Federal regulations and authority during national emergencies.

Some agencies are charged with enforcing specific statutes passed by a legislative body and given little discretion in their actions. Public health agencies are generally delegated broad authority and wide discretion to develop regulations and enforcement policies based on their expertise and the nature of a public health emergency. When these regulations are published and adopted by the agency, they have the force of law *unless they exceed the agency's statutory authority.*

The most important regulatory authority delegated to public health agencies is the power to act quickly and flexibly—without promulgating formal regulations and without judicial hearings— when necessary to respond to exigent circumstances and to prevent abuse, hearings and other review proceedings that interfere with efforts to ensure the public's health or after the action has been taken.

More commonly, however, public health agencies promulgate specific regulations or adopt national codes as binding in their jurisdiction. These are enforced through licensing, demonstrations of competency, and/or other mechanisms that require regulated entities to adhere to the regulations. This provides clear guidance for the regulated entities, ensures a timely response during a public health emergency, and simplifies enforcement.

Deviations from the standards are easily documented, which may prevent lengthy legal challenges to enforcement actions and ease efforts to review the decision circumstances of the event.

For more information, see Richards, E. P., and Rathbun, K. C. (1998). "Public Health Law." In *Maxcy-Rosenau-Last Public Health and Preventive Medicine,* ed. R. B. Wallace. Stamford, CT: Appleton and Lange.

Typical Role of the Federal Government during a Pandemic

The Federal government is responsible for nationwide coordination of the pandemic influenza response.

Specific areas of responsibility include the following:

1. Surveillance in the United States, territories, and globally
2. Epidemiologic investigation in the United States, territories, and globally
3. Development and use of diagnostic laboratory tests and reagents
4. Development of reference strains for vaccines
5. Vaccine evaluation and licensure
6. Determination of populations at highest risk and strategies for vaccination/antiviral use
7. Assessment of measures to decrease transmission (e.g., travel restrictions, isolation, and quarantine)
8. Deployment of federally purchased vaccine
9. Deployment of antiviral agents that may be available as part of the Strategic National Stockpile
10. Evaluation of the efficacy of response measures
11. Evaluation of vaccine safety

12. Deployment of the Commissioned Corps Readiness Force (CCRF) and Epidemic Intelligence Service (EIS) officers
13. Medical and public health communications
14. Activation and deployment of additional regional, federal and Department of Defense resources

Typical Role of State Division of Public Health Before and During a Pandemic

1. Establishment a state pandemic planning executive committee
2. Advocate the importance of pandemic planning to relevant decision-makers
3. Periodically update plan in close collaboration with relevant partners, including those outside the health sector, and with reference to current WHO and CDC guidelines
4. Ensure implementation of planning and preparedness activities at all levels of public authorities
5. Exercise influenza pandemic plans and use the results to improve and refine plan and preparedness
6. Identify crucial gaps in state and/or local infrastructure and resources, laws and/or statutes, which, if not corrected in advance, may interfere with an effective response
7. Develop and maintain lists, including contact information, of partners, resources, and facilities
8. Identify, brief regularly, and train key personnel to be mobilized in case of the emergence of a new strain of influenza virus
9. Coordinate planning with bordering jurisdictions, including counties, states, and unique populations (such as new immigrant and refugee populations, and certain religious sectors)

Planning for Schools and Centers

10. Consider the development of a state stockpile (antivirals, personal protective equipment, vaccines, laboratory diagnostics, and other technical support) for rapid deployment when needed
11. Ensure procedures for rapid sharing of specimens or isolates for virus characterization and development of diagnostics and vaccine
12. Develop surge capacity contingency plans for the internal management of state resources and essential workers during a pandemic

Influenza statewide surveillance: Some states include several major components. The following is an example:

- o Surveillance for influenza-like illness (ILI): Sentinel health-care providers from private practices, clinics, hospitals, and university health services report the number of patient visits for influenza-like illness (ILI: defined as fever and sore throat or a cough) by age group and the total number of patient visits each week. These providers send specimens from patients with ILI to the state public health for viral isolation and typing. A sample of these isolates is sent to CDC for further strain characterization.
- o Virologic surveillance: (some state departments of public health have

Planning for Schools and Centers

collaborating laboratories that report the number of clinical specimens tested for influenza and the number of positive results by virus type and subtype). Hospital laboratories that are part of the National Respiratory and Enteric Viruses Surveillance System (NREVSS) also report the number of clinical specimens tested for influenza and the number of positive results by virus type and subtype. Additional hospital laboratories report the number of clinical specimens tested for Respiratory Syncytial Virus (RSV) and the number of positive results.

o Surveillance for influenza and pneumonia-associated deaths: The Vital Statistics Offices in states report the percentage of total deaths caused by influenza and pneumonia each week.

o Influenza-associated pediatric and adult hospitalizations: The Emerging Infections Program (EIP) is monitoring influenza-associated hospitalizations among children and adults in in hospitals.

o Influenza-associated pediatric deaths: Deaths are reported through a state surveillance system.

o State influenza activity level: Each week, the state epidemiologist or designee reports

influenza activity as "widespread",
"regional", "local", "sporadic", or "none"
based on the surveillance systems described
above and additional existing bioterrorism
or syndromic surveillance systems available
at the time.

o Hospital Emergency Departments: Hospitals
report increases in the number of
symptomatic patients. Chief complaints are
categorized into syndromes (e.g.
gastrointestinal, rash, and respiratory) and
analyzed using the CDC Early Aberration
Reporting System (EARS).

o Emergency Medical Services (EMS): Data
from EMS calls are collected through "First
Watch," a web-based surveillance system.

o Schools Absenteeism: School enrollment
and absenteeism data from some schools,
centers, and/or districts are collected and
analyzed on a weekly basis.

o Over-the-counter drug sales: Pharmacy data
are collected through the University of
Pittsburgh Real-time Outbreak and Disease
Surveillance (RODS).

o Pneumonia surveillance: EIP conducts
unexplained pneumonia surveillance,
including information on health-care
workers and international travelers.

Planning for Schools and Centers

In some states, surveillance communication is sent from public health. The following is an example:

- o Notify providers of the start of the influenza season
- o Send influenza report to District health offices, Sentinel providers, and other interested parties (weekly during influenza season and as often as necessary after influenza season).
- o Post updated influenza surveillance data on the Epidemiology Branch website.
- o Advertise the availability of influenza surveillance information on the Epidemiology Branch website.

In some places, state funds are used to purchase influenza vaccine for VFC-eligible children only. The vaccine is sent at no cost to public health clinics and private providers.

- o Some public health clinic information is posted on state public health websites.
- o Vaccine recommendations are sometimes posted on the public health websites.
- o Vaccine coverage estimates are derived from the Behavioral Risk Factor Surveillance System.

Educate public and providers on human influenza.

- o Fact sheet and FAQ on are commonly found on public health websites, including information on:
- o Influenza Outbreak Prevention and Control for LTCFs
- o Influenza Outbreak Prevention and Control for Schools
- o Provide media with periodic press releases
- o Post surveillance data to DPH website

Typical Role of State Emergency Management Agency Emergency Response – Pandemic

The Federal Department of Homeland Security (DHS) and local State Departments of Homeland Security – have an established threat condition level scheme. Threat conditions levels may change during a pandemic.

Each state emergency management agency has developed a protocol and established a Standard Operation Plan that clarifies the authority of the Governor and when to activate and operate the State Emergency Operations Center during a declared emergency.

Typically the State Emergency Management Agency will identify Essential State Functions (ESF) that corresponds with Essential Federal Functions (EFF), depending on the infrastructure of the state and the unique features and assets of the each state.

These ESFs will almost always include healthcare (including hospitals and ambulance services), mass transportation (including all aspects of transportation), law enforcement, fire and hazardous material suppression, environmental protection, logistics, governor's office, public information and communications, mental health care, workforce development, agriculture (food access and storage, water authority, sewer authority, and budget and finance.

Some states will include other infrastructure representatives that are unique to the state, such as the Port Authority, Airport Authority, private transportation, etc., with the understanding that the management of assets during an emergency such as a pandemic are under the control of the emergency management authority. Restitution issues need to be addressed as soon as possible.

Typical Role of the State Departments of Education Before, During, and After a Pandemic

State departments of education have committed to work with schools to assist in the development of local pandemic plans and to serve as a resource for school districts. Most state departments of education websites have a link to the United States Department of Health and Human Services Pandemic Information and other links so that school can find pertinent information as they develop pandemic plans and as they respond to a pandemic event.

State departments of education and private school associations encourage schools to promote prevention and education. "Good Hygiene" posters, flyers, and pamphlets are available at ***www.pandemicflu.gov***. School, family, and business pandemic checklists are available, also, at the same website. Additionally, state departments of education and state public health departments include pandemic information on their websites.

During a pandemic event, many state departments of education create an event webpage with the latest information from state and national public health, including school closure guidance from CDC. These web pages are typically updated as events develop.

Depending on circumstances, the state departments of education may activate an Incident Command Center (ICC), based on the guiding principles outlined in the National Incident Management System. Usually, state department of education staff members go to the ICC to represent essential services.

Each department may designate a backup staff member to represent the department in the event the primary staff member is unavailable.

Staff members from the following divisions within the state education departments usually participate with the ICC:

- ❖ Instruction
- ❖ Transportation
- ❖ Finance and Business Operations
- ❖ Support Services
- ❖ Human Resources
- ❖ Legal Services
- ❖ Food Services
- ❖ Technology
- ❖ Facilities
- ❖ Policy
- ❖ Public Information
- ❖ Assessment
- ❖ Title Programs

Many of the state departments of educations' ICC become operational based on the recommendation of the State or Local Emergency Management Agency or the State Division of Public Health, or when the Education Commissioner decides that circumstances support activation of the ICC.

Planning for Schools and Centers

A direct communication link is often established and remains open at all times with the Governor's office, Division of Public Health, and EMA.

The state department of education ICC communicates with the Emergency Operations Center (EOC), and when appropriate, send state department of education staff to the EOC. The state department of education's ICC establishes a telephone hotline, event website, and other means of communication in the ICC to receive inquiries from local school and to share information with a local school.

When appropriate, the state department of education information is shared with other state agencies and the news media via press release or website. *It is important to note that the local board of health will contact the local schools when a pandemic flu case has been confirmed in the district.*

A protocol is in place in most state departments of education to respond to unique and emergency-based situations in the state that impact local schools. At the Education Commissioner's discretion, local school requests, such as waivers, may be addressed through the ICC, or by an ad hoc committee. Some issues, such as employee sick leave accrual, payroll, etc. may require a legal decision.

The state departments of education are in direct contact with the decision-makers and should be prepared to share findings and decisions with the State Board of Education and local school districts expeditiously. Such decisions are based on emergency conditions and the best interests of

Planning for Schools and Centers

students, parents, employees, communities, and the State of State.

During an emergency, the state department of education's ICC maintains an archive of school requests and reports for reasons of follow-up, for referrals to appropriate state agencies, for future reference, and for document recovery necessary to file reimbursement claims with the Federal Emergency Management Agency.

The state department of education's ICC may provide technical assistance to LEAs regarding IEP-related issues. Many the state department of education Public Information Officer (PIO) coordinate all communications with other agencies through direct contact with agency PIOs to ensure that information is consistently communicated between and among agencies and to the public.

Several of the state departments of education utilize websites to disseminate educational content and serve as a link to technology-based educational websites to assist schools and parents in providing education during school closure due to a pandemic. The state departments of education work closely with public broadcasting to disseminate information.

State Department of Education and Local School Continuity of Operations Plan (COOP)

Most Continuity of Operations Plan (COOP) includes teleworking and technological improvements in employee-to-employee communications during a pandemic or other widespread emergency event. The following is an example.

1. Plans are implemented to allow more employees to telework, and the flexibility of work hours has been expanded. Essential positions and personnel have been identified and cross-training is in progress in those departments.
2. The Information Technology Division of the state department of education establishes a security and staffing emergency plan.
3. The Department of Human Resources often times develops a protocol to monitor staff attendance before, during, and after a pandemic event. This coupled with the expansion of teleworking and flexible work hours will aid recovery and resumption of operations after a pandemic event.
4. All suppliers of services and goods to state departments of education and local schools should establish an emergency response business operations plan, including consultants.

Decision-Making Matrix

All state agencies should work together to ensure that the state's preparation and response to a pandemic at all stages will be a coordinated effort within the operational principles of incident management.

It is not fully possible to determine all of the issues that may arise during a pandemic, particularly those that are related to the severity and duration of a pandemic and the difficult decisions that have to be made in a timely fashion.

The following Decision-Making Matrix is an example of how and who makes critical decisions at the state level during a pandemic.

This is an example of how a state tried to clarify the roles of state agencies during a pandemic. This is a brief summary and is not intended to supplant more detailed information that can be found in comprehensive state plans.

NOTE: School closure decisions are difficult to make because the decision impacts thousands of students, employees, parents and even businesses and service providers. Oftentimes, the decision to close a school due to an epidemic or pandemic is made by local and state education leaders, based on public health information.

The following is an example of a state's Decision- Making Matrix. It does not include all contingencies or scenarios. It is only presented here as an example.

Event	State Decision-Maker	District Health Dept. Actions	DPH Actions	EMA Actions	DOE Actions
Animal flu subtype poses human risk		Strengthen pandemic preparedness includes schools	Strengthen pandemic preparedness includes DOE	Strengthen pandemic preparedness	Strengthen pandemic preparedness communicate with DPH and EMA
Small cluster with limited human-to-human trans-mission, localized	DPH-Division Director	Conduct inventory of space and resources; review current emergency plans; educate staff; vaccine coverage; communicate with school district	Internal planning; notifications; enhance surveillance if identified in North America; communicate with DOE	Advise key personnel; notifications if identified in North America	Advise key personnel; notify school districts if identified in North America; communicate with DPH and EMA
Larger clusters, the virus is better adapted to humans	DPH-Division Director	Notify hospitals, boards of health, local EMAs, agencies, school districts, and NGAs	Notification; coordination; surveillance; EOC activation; plan for vaccine delivery and vaccination	Notification and State EOC activation planning; public messages; Confirmation of vaccine delivery plan	Advise key personnel; update schools; ICC activation planning; create information website; daily communication

Planning for Schools and Centers

Event	State Decision-Maker	District Health Dept. Actions	DPH Actions	EMA Actions	DOE Actions
Pandemic: increased and sustained spread of the virus	DPH-Division Director	Review plan for distribution of public sector vaccine; assist partners in vaccination availability	Internal activation; notification; coordination; enhance surveillance; vaccine delivery and vaccination	Activate State EOC; notifications	Activate ICC; update school districts; update information website; communicate with DPH and EMA
Further spread of virus across the world; formal decision to declare pandemic event	Governor (could include social distancing and partial or full closures)	Coordinate use of local resources; communicate with DPH, OHS-EMA; communicate with partners and assist partners in providing vaccine and antivirals, when available; communicate with school districts	Internal activation; notifications; communicate with partners; coordination; surveillance; planning and assessment; vaccine delivery; develop disease control and prevention protocols; establish information hotline; communicate with DOE	Notification; activate State EOC; coordinate state agency responses and communication; respond to needs of local emergency management; establish information hotline	Activate ICC; communicate with school districts; establish information hotline for school districts; coordinate and communicate with State EOC and DPH; serve to communicate public health information to school districts as needed by public health

Planning for Schools and Centers

Event	State Decision-Maker	District Health Dept. Actions	DPH Actions	EMA Actions	DOE Actions
Return of virus activity within weeks or months following the initial wave of infection	DPH Division Director	Coordinate use of local resources; communicate with DPH, OHS-EMA; communicate with partners and assist partners in delivery of vaccine and antivirals, when available; communicate with school districts	Internal activation; notifications; communicate with partners; coordination; surveillance; planning and assessment; vaccine delivery and administration; develop disease control and prevention protocols; establish information hotline; communicate with DOE	Notification; State EOC; coordinate state agency responses and communication; respond to needs of local emergency management-establish information hotline	ICC; communicate with school districts; continue information hotline for school districts; coordinate and communicate with State EOC and DPH; serve to communicate public health information to school districts as needed by public health
Cessation of pandemic and to recovery	DPH Division Director	Assess local capacity to resume normal public health functions; assess local response; communicate with school districts	Internal planning; notification; retrospective studies; evaluate response; review state plan, communicate with DOE	Notification; deactivate State EOC unless needed to aid local and state recovery; evaluate response	Deactivate ICC unless needed to aid school districts; assess waiver requests; continue information hotline for school districts

Pandemic Planning References and Resources

1. Broward County School District, *Pandemic Plan for Schools, www.browardschools.com*

2. California Contra Costa Health Services *www.cchealth.org*

3. Centers for Disease Control and Prevention, *Interim Pre-Pandemic Planning Guidance, www.pandemicflu.gov*

4. United States Department of Education, *Pandemic Planning www.ed.gov*

5. DeKalb County School District, *Pandemic Management Plan, www.dekalb.k12.ga.us*

6. State Department of Public Health, *Pandemic Influenza Plan for State, www.health.state.ga.us*

7. Iowa Department of Public Health, *Pandemic Influenza Planning guide for Iowa Schools, www.idph.state.ia.us*

8. Metro-Atlanta School Districts Pandemic Planning Sub-Committee, *Decision Matrix*

9. State of New Hampshire, *Influenza Pandemic Public Health Preparedness & Response Plan, www.dhhs.nh.gov*

10. Virginia Department of Education, *Pandemic Planning Guide for Schools, www.pen.k12.va.us*

Appendix

Influenza Risk Assessment Tool (IRAT)

The Influenza Risk Assessment Tool (IRAT) is an evaluation tool developed by CDC and external influenza experts that assesses the potential pandemic risk posed by influenza A viruses that currently circulate in animals but not in humans. The IRAT assesses potential pandemic risk based on two different scenarios: "emergence" and "public health impact."

"Emergence" refers to the risk of a novel (i.e., new in humans) influenza virus acquiring the ability to spread easily and efficiently in people. "Public health impact" refers to the potential severity of human disease caused by the virus (e.g., deaths and hospitalizations) as well as the burden on society (e.g., missed workdays, strain on hospital capacity and resources, and interruption of basic public services) if a novel influenza virus were to begin spreading efficiently and sustainably among people.

The IRAT uses 10 scientific criteria to measure the potential pandemic risk associated with each of these scenarios. These 10 criteria can be grouped into three overarching categories: "properties of the virus," "attributes of the population," and "ecology & epidemiology of the virus." Influenza subject matter experts evaluate novel influenza viruses based on each of these 10 criteria.

Each of the 10 criteria is then weighted statistically based on its significance to each of the two scenarios. A composite score for each virus is then calculated based on the given scenario. These composite scores provide a means to rank and compare influenza viruses to each other in terms of their potential pandemic risk for each of the two scenarios.

As we learn more about influenza A viruses, these 10 criteria may change, other criteria may be added or some current criteria may be dropped. The IRAT is designed to be flexible and responsive to current scientific advances.

What is the purpose of the IRAT?

The IRAT is intended to do the following:

- Prioritize and maximize investments in pandemic preparedness by helping to determine which novel (new) influenza viruses to develop vaccines against and capitalizing on surveillance efforts and in-country capacity building activities.

- Identify key gaps in information and knowledge which can be the basis to prompt additional studies. (For example, if information is not available for one of the 10 criteria used by the IRAT additional studies could be done or resources allocated to provide the needed information).

- Document in a transparent manner the data and scientific process used to inform management decisions associated with pandemic preparedness.

- Provide a flexible means to easily and regularly update the risk assessment of novel influenza viruses as new information becomes available.

- Be an effective communications tool for policy makers and the influenza community.

- Provide a means to weigh the 10 evaluation criteria differently depending on whether the intent of the risk assessment is to measure the ability of an influenza virus to "emerge" as a pandemic capable virus (i.e., become capable of efficient human-to-human spread) or "impact" the human population if it did emerge.

What are the evaluation criteria used by the IRAT?

The IRAT consists of 10 evaluation criteria grouped into three overarching categories. These categories and criteria are described as follows:

- The **"Properties of the Virus"** category contains four of the 10 evaluation criteria, including:

  1. **Genomic variation** is a measure of the extent of genetic diversity or presence of known molecular signatures important for human infections and disease.

  2. **Receptor binding** refers to the host preference (e.g., animal or human) of an influenza virus as well as the types of tissues and cells the virus is best suited to infecting (e.g., nose tissue and cells vs. deep lung tissue and cells). Some influenza viruses are better adapted to infecting humans as opposed to animals.

  3. **Transmission in lab animals** is a measure of the ability of an influenza virus to transmit efficiently in

animals in laboratory studies. Some influenza viruses can transmit through the air via small infectious droplets expelled through coughs or sneezes, whereas other influenza viruses may only spread through direct contact with an infected host.

4. **Antiviral treatment susceptibility/resistance** is a measure of how well an influenza virus responds to treatment with influenza antiviral drugs, such as oseltamivir, zanamivir, and M2 blockers.

The "Attributes of the Population" category contains three of the 10 evaluation criteria, including:

5. **Existing population immunity** refers to whether the human population has any existing immune protection against the novel influenza virus being evaluated. Susceptibility to infection and severity of illness associated with specific influenza viruses may depend on age, geographic area, or genetic factors.

6. **Disease severity and pathogenesis** measures the severity of illness caused by a particular influenza virus in people and/or animals.

7. **Antigenic relationship to vaccine candidates** is a measure of how similar a novel influenza virus is when compared to a current or previously manufactured influenza vaccine strain.

The "**Ecology and Epidemiology**" category contains the final three evaluation criteria, including:

8. **Global distribution (animals)** measures of how widespread an influenza virus is in animals. For example, is the virus found in animals in a limited area or is it found in animals from many different areas?

9. **Infection in animal species** refers to what kinds of animals are impacted by the influenza virus and the likelihood of human contact with these animals. For example, are influenza infections occurring in wild birds or domestic birds?

10. **Human Infections** determines whether human infections with a novel influenza virus are occurring. If so, under what circumstances are human infections occurring? For example, has human-to-human transmission or clusters of the disease occurred? Alternatively, how frequently and easily does transmission occur after direct and prolonged contact between humans and infected animals?

How are the IRAT's 10 evaluation criteria ranked and weighted?

Each of the 10 evaluation criteria provided in the IRAT tool is used by influenza experts to generate point scores estimating the potential pandemic risk associated with that criterion.

The point scores fall into three general classifications of risk: **low risk, moderate risk,** and **high risk**.

- "**low risk**" is associated with a point score between 1 and 3

- "**moderate risk**" is associated with a point score between 4-7

- "**high risk**" is associated with a point score between 8-10.

Each of the 10 evaluation criteria also is weighted according to importance to each of the two scenarios: **emerging** and **public health impact**.

When assessing an influenza virus for "emerging," the question asked is: **"What is the risk that a novel virus has the potential for sustained human-to-human transmission?"**

The evaluation criteria may be ranked and weighted as follows (with the first criterion receiving the highest rank and weight score, and the last criterion receiving the lowest rank and weight score).

- Human infections
- Transmission in lab animals
- Receptor binding
- Existing population immunity
- Infection in animal species
- Genomic variation

- Antigenic relationship to vaccine candidates
- Global distribution (animals)
- Disease severity and pathogenesis
- Antiviral treatment susceptibility/resistance

As an additional example, when assessing an influenza virus for "public health impact," the question asked is: "If the virus were to achieve sustained human-to-human transmission, what is the risk that a novel virus has the potential for significant impact on public health?"

The same evaluation criteria could be ranked and weighted as follows (with the first criterion receiving the highest rank and weight score, and the last criterion receiving the lowest rank and weight score).

- Disease severity and pathogenesis
- Existing population immunity
- Human Infections
- Antiviral treatment susceptibility/resistance
- Antigenic relationship to vaccine candidates
- Receptor binding
- Genomic variation
- Transmission in lab animals
- Global distribution (animals)
- Infection in animal species

Pandemic Preparedness Tools

Resources to help administrators and state and local health officials prepare for the next influenza pandemic. Some of the software listed below is primarily for public health specialists, but they contain elements and information can be very useful for schools and center pandemic planners.

- **Software: CommunityFlu 2.0**
  (http://www.cdc.gov/flu/pandemic-resources/tools/communityflu.htm)
  The software is designed to enable public health officials, policymakers, and students of infectious diseases to examine the spread of influenza pandemic through a community. *CommunityFlu* is a software program that simulates the spread of influenza through a model community, and the impact of a variety of potential interventions (e.g., vaccinations, school closings, wearing of face masks, patient and household isolation/self-quarantine). *CommunityFlu* can also be used to calculate the cost, in terms of workdays lost, of influenza and the associated interventions.

  CommunityFlu is an "individual agent" model, which means that it tracks, on a daily basis, the transmission of influenza among each individual person that populates a representative community.

  CommunityFlu tracks, for each person, their daily contacts in a variety of locales such as home, school, and workplace. Each contact represents a chance for the disease to spread from an infectious person to a disease susceptible person.

The representative community in the program comprises approximately 1,000 households with 2,500 persons. Each person in *CommunityFlu's* community belongs to a household or a long-term care facility. Depending upon age, a member can attend a daycare center, school, or workplace. School age children in the *CommunityFlu* community, for example, may attend one of four elementary schools, two middle schools, or one high school.

- **Software: FluAid 2.0**
  (http://www.cdc.gov/flu/pandemic-resources/tools/fluaid.htm)
  The software is designed to help state and local public health officials plan, prepare, and practice for the next flu pandemic.

- **Software: FluSurge 2.0**
  (http://www.cdc.gov/flu/pandemic-resources/tools/flusurge.htm)
  The software is a spreadsheet-based model that provides hospital administrators and public health officials with estimates of the surge in demand for hospital-based services during the next flu pandemic.

- **FluLabSurge 1.0**
  (http://www.cdc.gov/flu/pandemic-resources/tools/flulabsurge.htm)
  The spreadsheet-based program is designed to assist laboratory directors forecast demand for specimen testing during the next influenza pandemic (i.e., the surge in demand), and develop response plans.

- **Software: FluWorkLoss 1.0**
  (http://www.cdc.gov/flu/pandemic-resources/tools/fluworkloss.htm)
  The software estimates the potential number of days lost from work due to an influenza pandemic. Pandemic influenza can overwhelm a community, causing very serious public health, social, and economic problems.

  Over a period of 30 years, between 1976 and 2006, estimates of influenza-associated deaths in the United States range from a low of about 3,000 to a high of about 49,000 people. And, on average, more than 200,000 people are hospitalized in the United States each year due to complications related to seasonal influenza. However, because illness rates during a pandemic are likely to be 2-5 times higher than a typical influenza season, special planning for work loss during pandemics is critical to maintaining continuity of operations in a severe pandemic.

  - *FluWorkLoss* estimates the potential number of days lost from work due to an influenza pandemic. Users can change almost any input value, such as the number of workdays

  Planning for Schools and Centers

assumed lost when a worker becomes ill or the number of workdays lost due to a worker staying home to care for a family member. Users can also change the length and virulence of the pandemic so that a range of possible impacts can be estimated. *FluWorkLoss* provides a range of estimates of total work days lost, as well as graphic illustrations of the workdays lost by week and percentage of total workdays lost to influenza-related illnesses.

- **Instructions to Estimate the Potential Impact of the Next Influenza Pandemic Upon Locale Y Using 1918 and 1968 Pandemic Scenarios[467 KB, 42 pages]** (http://www.cdc.gov/flu/pandemic-resources/tools/downloads/pandemic-impact-estimate-instructions.pdf)
  The tool includes basic instructions for the software programs *FluAid* and *FluSurge* as well as a template of a draft report.

Pandemic Preparedness Checklist

Citizens, schools, and centers can take a number of steps to prepare for a pandemic (or other types of emergencies) where typical access to supplies and services are interrupted or cut off. The following is a partial list of possible preparations, as suggested by the CDC and other agencies:

- o Store a two-week supply of water and food. During a pandemic, if you cannot get to a store, or if stores are out of supplies, it will be important for you to have extra supplies on hand. This can be useful in other types of emergencies, such as power outages and disasters.
- o Periodically check your regular prescription drugs to ensure a continuous supply in your home.
- o Have any nonprescription drugs and other health supplies on hand, including pain relievers, stomach remedies, cough and cold medicines, fluids with electrolytes, and vitamins.
- o Get copies and maintain electronic versions of health records from doctors, hospitals, pharmacies and other sources and store them, for personal reference. HHS provides an online tool intended to help people locate and access

their electronic health records from a variety of sources. http://healthit.gov/bluebutton

o Talk with family members and loved ones about how they would be cared for if they got sick, or what will be needed to care for them in your home.

o Volunteer with local groups to prepare and assist with emergency response.

o Get involved in your community as it works to prepare for an influenza pandemic.

Precautions During a Pandemic

The CDC and the National Institutes of Health report that a number of steps can be taken to lessen the spread of a pandemic. This is a partial list of recommendations.

- **Avoid close contact** with people who are sick. When you are sick, keep your distance from others to protect them from getting sick too.
- If possible, **stay home** from work, school, and errands **when you are sick.** You will help prevent others from catching your illness.
- **Cover your mouth and nose** with a tissue when coughing or sneezing. It may prevent those around you from getting sick.
- **Washing your hands** often will help protect you from germs.
- **Avoid touching your eyes, nose or mouth.** Germs are often spread when a person touches something that is contaminated with germs and then touches his or her eyes, nose, or mouth.
- **Practice other good health habits.** Get plenty of sleep, be physically active, manage your stress, drink plenty of fluids, and eat nutritious food.

Traveling Out of the Country When Pandemic Emerges

When staff members, volunteers, students, and family members are traveling out of the country they need to rely on local healthcare providers and locally-available medications.

United States Government facilities overseas, such as Embassies, Consulates, and military facilities, lack the legal authority, capability, and resources to dispense vaccines, medications, or medical care to private U.S. citizens.

They need to consider local conditions and evaluate your ability to maintain adequate supplies of food, water, and medication. Decide where would be safest during a pandemic and plan accordingly.

Ask doctors and health insurance companies in advance about how they could get appropriate medication for treatment if they become ill, keeping in mind it could take many months to develop and produce sufficient quantities of a vaccine during a worldwide pandemic.

Research the availability and quality of medical facilities at the destinations and consider purchasing medical evacuation insurance.

Be aware that hotels may cease to provide housekeeping and meal services during a severe pandemic, and many may close or steeply raise prices.

Consider changing travel plans or returning to the United States once there is evidence of sustained human-to-human transmission of a more severe form of influenza since commercial air transportation may quickly become unavailable.

In the event of a severe, global pandemic, you should be prepared to remain abroad longer than your planned trip. You should avoid non-essential travel beyond your residence and workplace. You should also limit activities that could expose you to others who may be ill.

Based on varying conditions abroad, you should prepare contingency plans and emergency supplies (non-perishable food, potable water or water-purification supplies, medications, etc.) for the possibility of remaining in that country up to twelve weeks.

Visit the U.S. Government's federal influenza website to see examples of comprehensive planning checklists for individuals, businesses, schools, and other groups.

Pandemic Influenza Health Tips

http://www.cdc.gov/germstopper/

Information for parents and school staff:

Protect yourself against the spread of the flu and other germs and viruses:

> • The main way illnesses like the flu and the common cold spread are by tiny droplets sprayed into the air when someone coughs or sneezes. Cover your nose and mouth with a tissue or your upper sleeve when coughing or sneezing. Throw away used tissues immediately.

> • Wash hands thoroughly and often. That means using soap and warm water and washing for 20 seconds. Use alcohol-based hand sanitizers when hand washing is not possible.

> • Avoid touching your eyes, nose or mouth. Germs are often spread when you touch something contaminated with germs. Germs can live for two hours or more on surfaces like doorknobs, desks, or chairs.

> • Avoid close contact with those who are sick.

> • Visit http://www.cdc.gov/germstopper/ for more information.

If you do come down with a cold or the flu, take these steps to get well:

- Wash your hands often.

- Stay home and keep your distance from others to protect them from getting sick, too.

- Get plenty of rest.

- Drink lots of fluids like water, tea, broth or juice.

- Take acetaminophen or ibuprofen as needed for pain or fever.

- Use a vaporizer or saline drops to relieve congestion.

SAMPLE PARENT LETTER: Prevention and Information
Use this letter to help prepare parents for pandemic flu before local cases are confirmed.

Dear Parents,

This letter will help your family prepare for a flu pandemic that could make many people sick. It is important to know that at this time there is **no** pandemic flu in our community.

However, public health officials are worried the flu virus may change so that it can infect people and spread easily from person-to-person. This may cause a widespread flu outbreak, called a pandemic.

Public health officials want people to protect themselves against pandemic flu. Here are some ways to protect your family:

✓ Keep children who are sick at home. Don't send them to school.

✓ Teach your children to wash hands with soap and water for 20 seconds. Be sure to set a good example by doing this yourself.

✓ Teach your children to cover coughs and sneezes with tissues or by coughing into the inside of the elbow. Be sure to set a good example by doing this yourself.

Planning for Schools and Centers

✓ Teach your children to stay at least three feet away from people who are sick.

✓ People who are sick should stay home from work or school and avoid other people until they are better.

Enclosed with this letter is a checklist to help families get ready for a pandemic flu outbreak. This information can also help your family get ready for any kind of emergency.

If you have questions, please contact your school nurse, healthcare provider, or your local board of health.

The federal government website with information on planning for individuals and families:
http://www.pandemicflu.gov
American Red Cross http://www.redcross.org
http://www.redcross.org

SAMPLE LETTER: Case in the United States
Use this letter to help prepare parents for pandemic flu after confirmation that the virus is spreading but is not yet in the local community.

Dear Parents,
A potential pandemic flu virus is now in the United States. Health officials are concerned that the flu virus may spread to several states. This would cause a widespread flu outbreak, called a pandemic. So even though there are no flu cases nearby, we want to remind you about some ways to protect your family from getting sick:

- ✓ Keep children who are sick at home. Don't send them to school.

- ✓ Teach your children to wash hands a lot with soap and water for 20 seconds. Be sure to set a good example by doing this yourself.

- ✓ Teach your children to cover coughs and sneezes with tissues or by coughing into the inside of the elbow. Be sure to set a good example by doing this yourself.

- ✓ Teach your children to stay at least three feet away from people who are sick.

✓ People who are sick should stay home from work or school and avoid other people until they are better.

We will keep you informed if the situation changes. Please know that we are in contact with the local board of health at all times.

Enclosed with this letter is a checklist to help families get ready for a pandemic flu outbreak. This information can also help your family get ready for any kind of emergency. If you have questions, please contact your school nurse, healthcare provider, or your local board of health.

The federal government website with information on planning for individuals and families:
http://www.pandemicflu.gov
The American Red Cross: *http://www.redcross.org*

SAMPLE LETTER TO PARENTS: Case in the state
Use this letter to give parents basic information about a pandemic flu outbreak and to inform parents that a flu virus is in the state but not in nearby schools.

Dear Parents,

This letter will give you information about a flu outbreak in [Insert county/city here]. This year there is a new flu virus that is making many people sick. So many people are sick that United States health officials call it a "pandemic flu." A flu virus case has been confirmed in State and in a State school district. We have no confirmed or probable cases in our school district. If this changes, we will follow the CDC guidance and inform you of any changes in school operations.

At this time, the county health department tells us that students who are not ill can safely come to school. The schools will remain open. We will keep you updated with any important information.

To keep the flu from spreading to more people, we ask you to keep sick children home. Any children who are sick in school will be sent home. Public health officials want you to protect yourself and your family against pandemic flu. Here are some ways to stop the spread of germs and sickness:

✓ Keep children who are sick at home. Don't send them to school.

✓ Teach your children to wash hands a lot with soap and water for 20 seconds. Be sure to set a good example by doing this yourself.

✓ Teach your children to cover coughs and sneezes with tissues or by coughing into the inside of the elbow. Be sure to set a good example by doing this yourself.

✓ Teach your children to stay away at least three feet away from people who are sick.

✓ People who are sick should stay home from work or school and stay away from other people until they are better.

If the pandemic flu continues to spread and more students become ill, schools may close. The purpose of closing schools will be to keep children from getting sick. If schools are closed, children should stay at home. Begin planning now for childcare in your home. Recommendations may change during the course of a pandemic flu outbreak.

Planning for Schools and Centers

If you have questions, please contact your school nurse or healthcare provider. You can call the school hotline (INSERT NUMBER). You may also contact the local health department (INSERT NUMBER or WEBSITE). The federal government has a website with information on planning for individuals and families: *http://www.pandemicflu.gov*, as does the American Red Cross: *http://www.redcross.org*

SAMPLE LETTER TO PARENTS and STAFF: Case in nearby County
Use this letter to inform parents that a flu virus is in a nearby county but not in your school.

Dear Parents/Guardians/Staff:
I hope you have taken the time to carefully review the letter from me regarding the flu that was distributed to all students and staff and is now posted on our website. As of this writing, there have been no confirmed cases of this flu in _____ County. However, there has been a confirmed case in _____ County.

At this time, local public health officials tell us that students can continue to safely attend classes and schools will remain open. The spread of the virus will be monitored closely in the coming days and we will follow recommendations of public health in response to any changes in the status of the virus which could affect our schools and community.

In the event there are confirmed cases in _____ County, we will work with public health officials to carefully evaluate necessary actions. If school closings become necessary, we will make every effort to inform our community immediately using our website, our education channel, and the media. Based on the circumstances, schools may be closed for days or weeks. Parents should begin now making plans for childcare in the event it is needed.

Please continue to implement the following measures to protect against the flu:

- Staying home from work or school and limiting contact with others when you are sick
- Covering your nose and mouth with a tissue when you cough or sneeze and properly discard used tissues. If no tissue is available, cough or sneeze into your upper sleeve, not your hands.
- Frequently washing your hands with soap and water or an alcohol-based hand sanitizer
- Avoiding touching your eyes, nose, and mouth. Germs spread this way.
- Avoiding close contact with those who are ill.

Up-to-date health information can be obtained at *www.cobbanddouglaspublichealth.org* and *www.cdc.gov/swineflu*.

SAMPLE LETER TO PARENTS: *Use this letter to inform parents of school closing due to possible exposure to virus.*

Dear Parents,

The _____health officials have recommended that _____ school(s) in _____ to close immediately. This order is because of the pandemic flu situation.

_____ school(s) is/are immediately closed until further notice and children should stay home. The school(s) may be closed for several days or weeks to reduce contact among children and stop the spread of the flu. We know this is a hard time for our community and our hearts go out to those who are ill.

We will remain in contact with you to update the status of the school(s). You may wish to check our school district web page for updated information and tune to local news stations for more information.

We know that it may be hard to get a doctor's appointment, go to a clinic or even be seen in a hospital emergency room. Here are some tips for helping those who are sick with the flu:

✓ Have them drink a lot of liquid (juice, water).

✓ Keep the sick person as comfortable as possible. Rest is important.

✓ For fever, sore throat and muscle aches, use ibuprofen (Motrin) or acetaminophen (Tylenol). Do not use aspirin with children or teenagers; it can cause Reye's syndrome, a life- threatening illness.

✓ Keep tissues and a trash bag within reach of the sick person.

✓ Be sure everyone in your home washes their hands frequently.

✓ Keep the people who are sick with the flu away from the people who are not sick.

For more information, call your healthcare provider or the local health department (insert number).

We will contact you as soon as we have information about when school will reopen, and we will inform the local news media.

We encourage all parents to encourage their children to read whatever textbooks are available at home, to read other reading material at home, to practice computations and writing while at home, and, if available, access instructional programs on the internet, network, public, and/or access channels.

Planning for Schools and Centers

SAMPLE LETER TO PARENTS: School Re-Opens

Use this letter to inform parents schools are re-opened.

Dear Parents,

The _____health officials have declared the pandemic flu is under control. Our school will open again on _____. At this time, students may safely return to class.

Even though school is opening, there are still some people who are sick from the flu virus. Health officials say that pandemic flu outbreaks sometimes happen in waves. This means more people could become sick soon again. If more people get sick, schools may need to close again. We will continue to give you any important information.

We are looking forward to seeing your children again. Please remain alert for any news media updates and periodically check the school district's website for updates or other pertinent information.

In the near future, we will provide you more information about how school days and school work missed during the school closure will be made up. We will also send you a revised school year calendar as soon as possible.

If your child has any physical or mental health needs because of the flu outbreak, please let your child's school counselor know as soon as possible.

Planning for Schools and Centers

If you have any questions, please contact the local board of health and/or the school district at the following phone numbers:

Public Health: _____

School District: _____

Sample Pandemic Flu Tabletop Exercises

The ultimate goal of a pandemic tabletop exercise is to provide school as well as their respective communities and public health partners an opportunity, through discussion of possible events, to better prepare for a pandemic flu outbreak. The following are examples from CDC.

Set up:

Use a meeting room that will hold up to 20 people. Set aside a half day to a day for the exercise. Bring in individuals you either have designated for leadership positions if your plans are in place or ones you believe would be important in the event of a pandemic event. Ask your local health department and emergency management personnel to participate in the setup of the exercise and to participate in the tabletop exercise. Consider including non-participating observers to make notes of the exercise. Consider allowing others including local hospital administration and Red Cross to evaluate the process and provide information or answer questions as needed.

Irrespective of your present level of planning, the exercise will lead to a list of priorities for addressing an event of this type. Many of the issues that will arise will be helpful for other "all hazards" preparedness planning. You will also be introduced to other "key partners" in the community who will also be affected by the event.

You can either present the entire scenario to participants or break out the particular modules and present them separately, in order, to participants as the scenario progresses. Adapt the scope and particulars as needed in relation to local circumstances. Set time limits for each module discussion.

Purpose:

1. To raise awareness of issues associated with a Pandemic Influenza Outbreak

2. To evaluate gaps in school plans

3. To begin the process of internalizing the scope and magnitude of a relatively 'worst case" pandemic influenza event

Objectives:

1. Illustrate the present level of Pandemic Preparedness Planning for your school.

2. Explain how priorities are established by an emergency planning committee during a Pandemic.

3. Illustrate the present level of interaction with local public health.

4. Describe the challenges associated with a pandemic flu event.

Narrative (baseline setting):

1. WHO (World Health Organization) has raised the Pandemic Alert level based upon evidence of sustained and increasing levels of human-to-human transmission.

2. CDC (Centers for Disease Control and Prevention) has issued travel restrictions and is encouraging public health entities to implement enhanced surveillance for patients who may have flu symptoms.

Module 1 – Setting:

1. Two weeks pass. Several patients have been laboratory confirmed to have the influenza virus that has been associated with the human-to-human transmission. These cases are initially identified on the East and West coasts of the United States.

2. CDC has issued Health Alerts to State and Local Public Health Departments urging them to take necessary public health measures to contain outbreaks.

3. Local and National media are running stories on flu cases and has increased concerns among the public.

Discussion

    a. What are the issues for your school and public health at this point in the scenario?

    b. What measures does your plan call for? Do you have a plan?

    c. Are your command and control systems in place (National Incident Management System based or other) to begin coordinating efforts?

    d. What communications have you had with your local public health authorities?

    e. How would you monitor and support your employees during this period of a pandemic?

    f. Is your external communications plan functioning? How do you think the media will report the event? How will you respond to their requests for information?

    g. What special or unique issues exist within schools that need to be anticipated and dealt with? (e.g. legal, technical, contractual,

Planning for Schools and Centers

teachers, students, nursing, maintenance, food service)

h. Of the issues that arise, which ones would apply to other crisis management situations?

i. How did you respond upon initially hearing of cases in other parts of the country?

j. Identify which elements of crisis response infrastructure you have in place and which ones you do not. What are your strengths and weaknesses? Use this as your baseline for the rest of the scenario.

Module 2 – Setting

1. Two more weeks pass. Your state health department confirms five cases of the virus have been reported within the state.

2. Local universities and other public schools are experiencing increased absentee rates. It is not known to what degree this is a self-quarantine situation or a result of actual illness.

3. The school nurse reports indications of symptoms in the student population in your school.

4. Teachers and other staff begin calling in reporting symptoms for themselves and/or their own children or family members and cannot report to work.

5. Hospitals are reporting shortages in Personal Protective Equipment (PPE) and staff. Once again, it is unknown how much of this is due to the virus, fear or rumor.

Discussion

a. What information do school and public health decision-makers need to know at this point?

b. How will the school district receive information from local public health?

c. How or can you obtain the information?

d. What measures would the school implement at this time?

e. How will you maintain continuity of operations during this phase?

f. Do you have a Continuity of Operations Plan?

Module 3 – Setting

1. After four weeks of widespread illness and an exponentially increasing number of cases, the public is fearful of going out into the community and public health has begun implementing "voluntary" community containment measures.

2. You receive reports that some students and staff have symptoms of the virus.

3. Local hospitals report several citizens are coming in with real or imagined virus symptoms.

4. Schools are being pressured to close by public health, but businesses, parents and others want the schools to remain open.

5. Supply systems for your school including food and maintenance are no longer functioning.

6. People within your family are sick and others are showing symptoms. Of the 10 people initially in your decision-making system, some are absent. You have not heard from and cannot contact two of them.

7. You have received an increasing number of calls from staff who have recovered from the flu.

Planning for Schools and Centers

Discussion

  a. Will schools be closed?

  b. Do you have an alternative to closing schools? (i.e., screening procedure)

  c. What is your criterion for closing or not closing the school?

  d. Does your plan include public health in the decision to close schools?

  e. If schools are closed, how and for how long? How will the announcement be made? How will employees know?

  f. What are your procedures for closing schools and securing buildings?

  g. What are your plans for educational continuity?

Summary

  1. Acknowledge that this scenario represents a "worst case" scenario and then decide if future exercises (after improvement actions are taken) should function at this or a "better case" level based upon existing planning estimates. This tabletop example

is primarily to provide a baseline for planning purposes.

    a. Discuss how well your local community response plans are coordinated.

    b. Explain how you would prioritize needs at various points during the event (modules).

    c. What role would, should or could the school and/or school system play within the local response to the event?

2. Describe logistical challenges associated with a pandemic flu event.

3. Knowing that there will likely be a second wave of the pandemic influenza coming, how will you prepare for that? What will be different? What will be the same in that event?

4. Provide an anonymous process evaluation form for participants and technical assistance providers to submit.

Additional Sample Questions to Guide a Tabletop Exercise for Pandemic Planning

1. What kind of educational material is available to faculty, staff, students and parents about pandemic influenza?

2. Does the plan outline the decision-making process, key personnel, and criteria for canceling classes or closing schools? For example, are decisions made by the education or health agency? At the state or local level? Or, collaboratively?

3. Have faculty, staff, community and emergency response partners been involved in providing input and feedback for crisis planning for schools?

4. Is the school district's current emergency response plan suited for a pandemic influenza outbreak?

5. Is there a communication plan for keeping schools informed of decisions regarding school scheduling and closures?

6. Does the school system have a surveillance system for absences? If so, is this system linked to the local health department or other health-related entity?

7. Does the school plan adequately address the maintenance of educational operations in the case of a pandemic? If so, what plan is in place for

maintaining continuity of instruction (internet-based, individual/group mentoring) for students?

8. What is the school procedure for school closure when a public health emergency has been declared?

9. To address the fear of a pandemic influenza outbreak, does the school district have the capabilities to provide psychological support for student and faculty/staff when needed?

10. Does the school have established communication protocols with parents, staff, community and emergency response partners, such as local health departments and media, before and during a public health emergency?

11. What is the school's plan to communicate with media for latest information dissemination?

12. What is the school's plan to communicate with public health during pandemic influenza outbreak?

13. What key procedures are in place to support the continuity of essential school operations, during a long term school closure? The following items should be considered during discussions:

    a. Air quality/HVAC system functions

    b. Decontamination

Planning for Schools and Centers

   c. Safe learning environment and alternative teaching and learning methods

   d. Payroll

   e. Line of Succession for all key staff

14. How much time/school days does the district need to prepare to reopen individual schools within the district? For example, how many days are needed to:

   a. Replenish cleaning and hygiene supplies;

   b. Assess, identify and prioritize the order of individual schools to reopen;

   c. Assess staff capacity, including substitutes (remember, nearby school district will also be recruiting substitutes);

   d. Inform and train staff on health and prevention issues;

   e. Inform parents of school reopening plans and procedures; and

   f. Inform, train and modify learning environment to meet the needs of available staff and healthy students at school alongside alternative strategies addressing those at home.

Planning for Schools and Centers

15. What is the school's plan to provide psychological support to faculty, staff, students and parents who have been in isolation for three months and are having difficulty re-adjusting to "regular life?"

16. What is the school's plan to maintain monitoring for a possible resurgence of the virus?

17. Does the emergency management plan provide protocols standards for decontaminating the buildings and standards providing a safe and healthy environment?

18. What kind of resources does a district need in order to rehabilitate the learning environment (i.e., what supplies and tool, how many staff members will be present, and how many days.) For example, if the school was used as a community facility, such as a makeshift hospital or clinic or vaccine distribution site, what are the procedures for sanitizing the facilities?

19. Does the district have agreements in place with local and/or State emergency response entities regarding decontamination processes and determinations of safety?

20. Does the plan provide criteria for students and staff re-entering the school community and recontamination prevention programs? For example, those who have been exposed in the last

seven days are not permitted to attend school. For those attending school, are there sufficient hand-washing supplies and information awareness campaigns preventing the spread of germs?

21. What are the school's procedures to maintain communication with parents, staff, community and public health in case the virus resurfaces?

22. What are the school's plan to provide psychological support for faculty, staff, and students due to influenza-related serious illnesses or fatalities?

23. Does the school plan adequately address key issues, such as school faculty and staff training in pandemic flu knowledge and handling high morbidity and/or mortality in schools, in dealing with a mass influenza outbreak?

24. What issues did you identify in your procedures that could hinder pan flu efforts?

25. Do the school and district emergency response plans adequately address key issues faced during a long-term school closure, including continuity of instruction, feasibility of feeding students in school meal programs, continuity of business operations (e.g., payroll) and leave policies for teachers?

26. Do the school procedures properly coordinate communication response activity among schools, community, and public health during a pandemic

influenza event? In your opinion, what can be done to maintain and coordinate communication during an emergency situation such as the pandemic influenza scenario presented in the exercise?

27. Does the plan discuss/include resources to the district and schools?

28. What are the roles and responsibilities of parents throughout the district's pandemic influenza plan? Do they participate in prevention-mitigation activities? Preparedness? Response? Recovery? Are parents involved in the decision to cancel classes? At what level are they engaged?

29. Overall, is the school capable of effectively and efficiently recovering from a mass influenza outbreak in order to resume a safe learning environment? Can the team identify methods for hastening the disinfectant process? What social distancing strategies can be added?

Tips for Parents/Guardians for Extended Stay at Home During a Pandemic

Plan for an extended stay at home during a flu pandemic:

- ✓ Ask your employer about how the business will continue during a pandemic.
- ✓ Ask your employer if you can work from home during a flu pandemic.
- ✓ Plan alternative child care in the event that schools are closed and parents are working.
- ✓ Plan for a possible reduction or loss of income, if you are unable to work or your place of employment is closed.
- ✓ Check with your employer or union about leave policies.
- ✓ Plan home learning activities and exercises. Have materials, such as books, on hand.
- ✓ Plan recreational activities that your children can do at home.

Items to have on hand for an extended stay at home - examples of non-perishable foods Health and emergency supplies:

- ✓ Ready to eat canned meats, fruits, vegetables, soups
- ✓ Prescribed medical supplies such as glucose and blood pressure monitoring
- ✓ Protein or fruit bars

Planning for Schools and Centers

✓ Dry cereal or granola
✓ Peanut butter and jelly
✓ Dried fruit, nuts, trail mix
✓ Crackers
✓ Canned juices
✓ Canned or jarred baby food
✓ Baby formula
✓ Soap and water or alcohol-based hand wash
✓ Medicines for fever, such as acetaminophen (Tylenol) or ibuprofen (Motrin)
✓ Thermometer
✓ Vitamins
✓ Fluids with electrolytes, such as Pedialyte®
✓ Bottled water
✓ Flashlight with extra batteries
✓ Portable radio with extra batteries
✓ Manual can opener
✓ Pet food
✓ Garbage bags
✓ Tissues, toilet paper, disposable diapers

If someone in your home develops flu symptoms:

✓ Encourage plenty of fluids to drink.
✓ Keep the ill person as comfortable as possible. Rest is important.
✓ For adults with fever, sore throat and muscle aches, use ibuprofen (Motrin) or acetaminophen (Tylenol)

Planning for Schools and Centers

- ✓ Do not use aspirin in children or teenagers; it can cause Reye's syndrome, a life- threatening illness.
- ✓ Sponging with tepid (wrist-temperature) water lowers fever only during the period of sponging. Do not sponge with alcohol.
- ✓ Keep tissues and a trash bag for their disposal within reach of the patient.
- ✓ All members of the household should wash their hands frequently.
- ✓ Keep other family members and visitors away from the person who is ill.

Emergency Readiness for School Nutrition Programs Should Pandemic Flu or Epidemic Flu Occur

Position:

Children attending schools should be assured of a healthy environment any time they are on school property. Proper supplies for good personal hygiene should be provided to limit the spread of bacteria and viruses. Appropriate cleaning supplies should be available and used properly to control and kill these biological agents. The school nutrition program should have emergency readiness guidelines in place that coordinate with the plan for the rest of the school and with the local health department and other local authorities, should pandemic/epidemic flu or any emergency situation occur.

Definitions:

Pandemic: An outbreak of a disease in many countries at the same time. A pandemic of influenza—or flu—occurs when a new flu virus rapidly spreads from country to country around the world. The swift spread of a pandemic flu happens because people are not immune to the new flu virus and an effective vaccine would take months to develop.

Epidemic: An outbreak of a disease that spreads rapidly and extensively by infection and affects many individuals in an area or a population at the same time.

Planning for Schools and Centers

Avian Flu: Also called bird flu, avian flu is a flu-like virus that primarily is found in birds, but has infected several humans in other countries. The fear is that the avian flu virus will mix with human flu viruses and produce a new type of flu to which humans have no immunity. This new virus could cause a pandemic flu and affect many countries.

Swine Flu: A respiratory disease of pigs infected by type A influenza viruses that cause regular outbreaks in pigs. People do not normally get swine flu, but human infections can and do happen. Swine flu viruses have been reported to spread from person-to-person.

Background

Research suggests that currently circulating strains of avian flu viruses are becoming more capable of causing disease in animals than were earlier avian flu viruses. The avian influenza A virus that emerged in Asia in 2003 continues to evolve and may adapt so that other mammals may be susceptible to infection as well. Many epidemiologists believe that it is only a matter of time before the avian flu virus mutates with the human flu virus to cause a pandemic (1).

Swine Influenza (swine flu) is a respiratory disease of pigs caused by type A influenza viruses that causes regular outbreaks in pigs. People do not normally get swine flu, but human infections can and do happen. Swine flu viruses have been reported to spread from person-to-person, but in the past, this transmission was limited and not sustained beyond three people.

In late March and early April 2009, cases of human infection with swine influenza A (H1N1) viruses were first reported in Southern California and near San Antonio, Texas. Other U.S. states have reported cases of swine flu infection in humans and cases have been reported internationally as well (3).

When pandemic/epidemic flu becomes apparent, it will probably be learned through media coverage before illness occurs in a particular area. This early warning will give time to do last minute preparations in accordance with the recommendations found here and local emergency procedures.

The school foodservice manager and staff are well trained in food safety and are assets to the implementation of a school's emergency plan. Each school has at least one nutrition staff member, usually the manager, who has successfully completed food safety certification training and an exam. This exam is nationally recognized and is usually the ServSafe exam administered by the National Restaurant Association.

While there are similar guidelines in any emergency plan for schools, there are unique measures that should be taken in the event of pandemic/epidemic flu. Few emergencies will have as widespread an effect as will pandemic/epidemic flu, both inside and outside the school.

Recommendations

Before the pandemic or epidemic occurs

1. Maintain, and update frequently, a list of all staff members with home addresses, e-mail addresses, phone numbers and emergency contact information.

2. Maintain a written record of all persons who have keys and access to kitchen and cafeteria entrances, walk-in coolers/freezers and dry storage areas.

3. Determine if vendors have a pandemic/epidemic or emergency plan for continuity or recovery of supply deliveries when an emergency occurs that reduces the workforce. If they do not have a plan, encourage them to do so.

4. Focus on prevention as the most important measure in stopping anyone from getting any contagious illness. For viruses like the flu, hand-washing is the number one preventive measure. Preparation in schools for pandemic flu or any contagious illness should include the provision of proper supplies in restrooms. Also, teach students the importance of hand-washing at all grade levels. Students should also be taught the importance of coughing and sneezing into their upper sleeve to avoid spreading bacteria and viruses. These measures are important for anyone in a school but are even more important

for those eating meals in school cafeterias. Good personal hygiene will help prevent the transfer of viruses from hand to mouth as food is consumed.

5. Be aware of the symptoms to look for—for your own health as well as that of others. The Centers for Disease Control and Prevention defines an influenza-like illness as having the following symptoms:

    a. A fever of 101.5°F or higher; and
    b. One of the following – a cough, sore throat, headache and/or muscle ache (2).

Nausea, vomiting, and diarrhea may accompany the above symptoms.

6. Once the flu gets to an area, schools will begin to see a gradual increase in absenteeism. At some point, predetermined by the school's emergency plan, parents will be notified of the increased absenteeism. When this occurs, there will probably be an immediate further increase in absenteeism because of the fear of being exposed to the flu. This alone will decrease the number of meals that need to be prepared. A daily update on student attendance will help the school nutrition manager estimate the amount of food preparation needed for each day.

Planning for Schools and Centers

7. Once pandemic flu becomes evident in the United States, the time for last minute preparation will not be long. Some preparations need to be done in advance, such as:

   a. Vendors may have to close due to staff shortages. A list of alternative vendors and contact information should be updated regularly

   b. Maintain at least a five-day supply of food products. These foods should include at least a two-day supply of products that can be easily served in bag lunches. In the event of a pandemic flu, a regular five-day supply will probably be enough for more than five days because of student absenteeism.

   c. There may be staff shortages in school nutrition. Plan to limit menu items and possibly provide bag lunches if necessary or if it will make the workload easier. Maintain enough disposable plates, cups, and utensils for five days use in case staff shortages make it difficult to operate the dish machine.

   d. Carefully maintain proper cleaning and sanitizing procedures and perform routine maintenance on equipment. Proper cleaning and sanitizing are always necessary, but it takes on increased importance when there is an illness outbreak. Dishwashing machines

Planning for Schools and Centers

must be maintained to operate according to the data plate on the front of the machine.

e. Update employee health guidelines to reflect the necessity for excluding employees from the facility should symptoms of a sore throat with fever, vomiting, and/or diarrhea occur. In addition, a required condition for reinstatement during a flu pandemic/epidemic must be written documentation from a health practitioner that the person is free of the flu causing virus.

f. Prevention is of primary importance, therefore, hand washing takes on increased significance. There are no hand sinks available in most school cafeteria dining areas. The second choice for hand sanitizing is hand sanitizer. Maintain a supply of hand sanitizer that will be enough for treating the average number of students coming to a cafeteria for five days. (Note: Even though some cafeterias may have an available hand sink for student hand washing, hand sanitizer is a good additional preventive measure.)

g. The most effective sanitizer for killing viruses is chlorine bleach. Maintain a supply of chlorine bleach for sanitizing cafeteria tables, seats, door knobs and other surfaces

Planning for Schools and Centers

(1/4 cup bleach to 1-gallon water). Note that school nutrition only purchases chlorine bleach and other supplies for use by school nutrition. Replace chlorine bleach with a new product at least once each year as the strength may weaken over time. If the school does not want to use chlorine bleach, an EPA-registered hospital disinfectant or a sanitizer that is EPA-registered and labeled for activity against bacteria and viruses may be substituted. Use the disinfectant or sanitizer according to the manufacturer's instructions.

   h. Train all staff to be aware of flu symptoms and what the school's emergency preparedness plan includes.

8. If delivery of milk becomes a problem, contact the state School Nutrition Program for alternate solutions.
9. All students should be required to apply hand sanitizer to his/her hands upon entering the cafeteria. It is suggested that a school nutrition employee or teacher stand at the entrance of the cafeteria to ensure that each student applies hand sanitizer properly.
10. Self-service salad bars and buffets should be discontinued during a flu outbreak. Viruses do not multiply in food, but it only takes a very small

Planning for Schools and Centers

number to make someone ill. If a student who is ill coughs or rubs his nose and then touches food or contaminates the food in another way, the next person to choose the same food item will be infected.

11. At some point, students who are showing no symptoms may be quarantined in classrooms, possibly until they can be taken home. Bag lunches will probably be the best solution to feeding these students. Sanitize the cart that is used to transport the bag lunches to each classroom with a chlorine bleach solution, at least daily (1/4 cup chlorine bleach per gallon of water), and allow to air dry (another product may be used as stated in 7. g. above if chlorine bleach is not purchased). Provide large garbage cans outside the occupied classrooms according to a number of children and amount of waste materials. Custodians should tie up garbage bags promptly and dispose of them as soon as possible after the meal period.

12. Custodians should be provided with chlorine bleach by the building administrator or maintenance department to sanitize desks, classroom doorknobs and handrails daily and properly sanitize an area should vomiting occur. A recommended procedure for sanitizing an area after someone vomits is attached to this position statement. It is recommended that the same procedures for cleaning an area contaminated with norovirus be used for a

virus causing the flu. If the cafeteria and/or other floor areas are carpeted, a steam cleaner is the best alternative to using chlorine bleach. If chlorine bleach is not preferred for sanitizing surfaces such as desktops and doorknobs due to the possibility of staining carpets, an EPA-registered hospital disinfectant or other EPA-registered sanitizer labeled for activity against bacteria and viruses may be substituted.

While a school is closed

1. Once the absenteeism rate reaches a certain point predetermined by a school's emergency plan and/or by the local health authority, a school may need to be closed. Maintain contact with school administration to know the status of the situation and when the school will be reopened. Under some circumstances, as in swine flu (H1N1), CDC guidance states that a school should close immediately even if only one student has a suspected or confirmed case. In that case, closing the school is recommended for up to 14 days. CDC may update its guidance periodically.

2. There may be a need for outside feeding programs similar to seamless summer nutrition programs if the school, in agreement with local emergency authorities, thinks it is appropriate. If a school is not already approved for a seamless summer nutrition program, contact the state School Nutrition

Program for approval. If any of the guidelines need to be altered due to the situation, contact the state School Nutrition Program to consult with USDA for a waiver. In an emergency situation, the state School Nutrition Program will make it a priority to gain approvals and waivers as quickly as possible. Many schools have the properly insulated equipment to transport foods, especially if they have summer programs or a catered food. If a school doesn't have the necessary equipment to maintain proper temperatures, the equipment can possibly be borrowed from local caterers or non-potentially hazardous foods can be provided in bag lunches. Note that local caterer will probably have reduced business during a time of pandemic/epidemic flu since one of the recommendations to the public is to stay home and not participate in large gatherings.

3. If outside feeding is not needed or there are not enough staff members to operate such a program and it appears that the school will be closed for more than a week, consider discarding refrigerated potentially hazardous foods that have been prepared on-site or commercially prepared and opened. In lieu of discarding, you may consider wrapping the food products securely, dating them properly and freezing. Fresh produce and milk should never be frozen. Discard any food that has a sell-by or use-by/expiration date within the projected length of closure time period. Always inventory and record

types and amounts of food products that are discarded on production records so that costs are reflected in the SNO state reports. Contact vendors to suspend deliveries until further notice.

4. Depending on circumstances and staff availability, continue daily monitoring temperatures of refrigerated equipment. Keep in mind that your personal safety and protection are most important. Do not worry about monitoring equipment if instructions have been given not to return to the school premises or for everyone to stay at home.

5. In the event that a school has an "immediate closing" with only one day or less notification, do as much as you can to secure food products as described in this paper, but above all else, secure facilities as you would at the end of any day and leave the premises. Your health is most important. It is recommended that managers take contact information with them so that any necessary phone calls to vendors and others can be done from another location.

Re-opening school

1. Contact all employees to find out their health status and availability to come back to work. A small staff may mean that a smaller menu will need to be served.
2. Contact all vendors to notify them of time and date the school plans to re-open and to find out when they can make deliveries.
3. All food contact surfaces should be cleaned and sanitized unless they were completely wrapped with plastic wrap or other secure material to prevent contamination.
4. Check all food products and discard when :
    a. Signs of being out of temperature (excess ice crystals are a sign of refreezing, unusual odors and coloration).
    b. Signs of vandalism and tampering.
    c. Food products have expired use-by/sell-by/expiration dates.
5. In the event of vandalism or tampering with food products or any area of the school kitchen and cafeteria, notify the school principal and the police.
6. If the school has been closed for more than two weeks and/or there is any evidence of food temperature abuse, vandalism, facility damage or pest infestation, contact the local health department to assist in the evaluation of food products and other food safety/sanitation concerns.

Planning for Schools and Centers

It is important to understand that some sanitizers commonly used in food service are better than others when disinfecting surfaces after a possible contamination by norovirus. Quaternary Ammonium and ethanol alcohol are lipophilic sanitizers and therefore are not very effective against single-stranded, non-enveloped RNA viruses, such as norovirus since they lack a lipid envelope to attack. Barker, et al., 2004, did a disinfection study using norovirus, and found that when an area is contaminated with fecal material, the area must first be wiped clean with detergent and water, and then followed by a disinfection with exposure to 5000 ppm hypochlorite solution for at least 5 minutes in order to completely eliminate norovirus. This would be equivalent to about 1/4 cup of chlorine bleach in 1 gallon of water. However, this concentration is much higher than recommended for sanitizing food contact surfaces in the Food Code and may damage many materials, so great care must be taken in using this disinfection procedure. If the area is a food contact area, this disinfection procedure must be followed by a second step.

If the contaminated area consists of food contact surfaces, the second step includes following the disinfection with a clear-water rinse, and a final wipe down with a sanitizing bleach solution, consisting of 200 ppm chlorine bleach (1 teaspoon chlorine bleach per gallon of water). There are other disinfectants that have been found to be effective against the feline calicivirus, which is genetically similar to the norovirus, but there is no assurance that the feline calicivirus is similar in biocide resistance characteristics to norovirus. For example, EPA has registered a 0.5% hydrogen peroxide solution against the feline calicivirus.

Recommendations for environmental disinfection for norovirus include the need to disinfect all heavy hand contact surfaces such as food preparation surfaces, self-service utensil handles, faucets, tables, chairs, counters, door handles, push plates, railings, elevator buttons, telephones, keyboards, vending machine keyboards, pens, pencils, casino chips, cards, slot machines and sports equipment. Public restroom surfaces, including faucet handles, soap dispensers, stall doors and latches, toilet seats and handles, and towel dispensers are also important heavy fecal contamination areas that require disinfection. When norovirus contamination is suspected, cleaning procedures that increase the aerosolization of norovirus should not be utilized, such as vacuuming carpets or buffing hard surface floors. Contaminated carpeting should be disinfected with a chemical disinfectant if possible, and then steam cleaned for a minimum 5-minute contact time at a minimum temperature of 170 degrees F.

When a food worker or patron vomits in a public area or food preparation area, the vomit should be treated as potentially infectious material and should be immediately covered with a disposable cloth, and doused with a disinfectant to reduce the potential airborne contamination. All individuals in the immediate area of the vomiting incident should be cleared from the area before the vomit is cleaned-up.

Cleaning staff should use disposable face masks, gloves, and aprons when cleaning up after a vomiting incident. Paper toweling or other toweling used to clean-up liquid vomit should be immediately placed in a sealed trash bag and properly disposed of.

Note: School foodservice preparation staff should never handle clean-up of any bodily fluids, including vomit.

Crisis Management Planning Information

A comprehensive approach to crisis management places a strong emphasis on prevention. It should include strategies that establish communication procedures with local emergency management, a review school design and use of space, the development of student management policies, and the creation of plans for training of staff members. Crisis management planning anticipates potential problems and establishes a coordinated response to minimize threats to the safety of students and staff members and manages stress and disruption in the schools. A crisis management plan should also be developed with the goal to prevent a crisis from escalating. While it is not possible to anticipate all events, at the basic level there are elements that should be included in every crisis management plan:

1. Staff members participation in planning

2. Planning for a wide range of potential crisis events

3. Establishing a communication and information network within the school, school district, and with emergency responders

4. Establishing a coordinated response

5. Organizing and conducting debriefing sessions

Crisis management is a time-sensitive and focused intervention designed to identify, respond to and manage a crisis, restore order, restore equilibrium, and restore safety.

Planning for Schools and Centers

Foundation and Framework for Planning and Response

The chances of managing a crisis are increased if there are school district level policies and procedures that function within the framework of best crisis management and response practices and are tailored to conditions requiring a specific set of responses and resources. The development of policies and procedures that are appropriate and relevant for a crisis environment may need to deviate from traditional policy and procedure templates, because of the unique circumstances of crisis situations.

Benefits of Policies and Procedures for Crisis Management Planning

Policies and procedures for crisis management and prevention provide benefits for students, parents, and the school district.

1. The procedures provide an organized, systematic method for preparing staff members and students for a crisis.

2. Staff members know what circumstances and how to respond to an impending or possible crisis and an active crisis.

3. Staff members are trained on how to operate collaboratively within specified guidelines to make

Planning for Schools and Centers

decisions and respond appropriately to stressful situations.

4. Staff members know what circumstances and how to seek resources, report problems, make decisions, and work together to respond to rapidly evolving situations.

5. Parents, news media, and other members of the community are informed of the school district's actions and plans to be prepared in the event of a crisis situation, including how to respond to a crisis.

6. Interagency agreements, particularly with emergency responders and those agencies and entities with crisis response assets, foster stronger collaborative relationships and lead to a comprehensive community-wide response and management of a crisis.

7. No set of policies and procedures can prevent litigation; however, establishing policies and procedures based on sound practices and procedures provides some margin of protection against liability.

Framework for Crisis Plan Development

A comprehensive crisis management plan should be designed to effectively address a range of potential crises by including provisions for prevention and intervention and crisis response.

Prevention and Intervention Procedures

Prevention and intervention procedures provide an organized process for identifying, assessing, and intervening in a crisis that may include a potential or imminent threat or risk to students or staff members. These procedures are designed to prevent or reduce risk to the health, safety, and welfare of students and staff members and should include at least the following:

1. Training on severe weather identification and response

2. Training on staff members roles and responsibilities during a crisis

3. Training of students and staff members to recognize warning signs of risk

4. Immediate, mandatory reporting of concerns and events

5. Systematic assessment of threats

Planning for Schools and Centers

6. Expedited access to school and/or community resources for appropriate prevention and/or intervention

Crisis Response Procedures

Crisis response procedures should focus on situations which involve threats to students and staff members, such as natural disasters, school violence, accidents, and other situations. Such procedures should emphasize a coordinated response and are designed primarily to preserve and protect life and reduce the possibility of collateral threats to safety. Policies and practices should include the development of interagency agreements that specify channels of communication, types of services, and areas of responsibility. Such agreements typically are established with public safety (i.e., local or regional emergency management, police department, sheriff's office, fire department, emergency services), mental health agencies (both public and private), and public health. Sometimes it is necessary to establish agreements with businesses for resources and assets and other potential providers, such as care management organizations.

Procedures and practices should be problem-focused interventions designed to quickly and efficiently assess the crisis, disseminate accurate information, restore equilibrium, and support productive, appropriate responses for the following purposes:

1. To train leaders to recognize potential hazards and communicate and coordinate an appropriate response with their staff members

2. To protect life

3. To train students and staff members to recognize warning signs of risk

4. To encourage timely reporting of concerns/observations

5. To expedite access to school and/or community resources for appropriate prevention and intervention

6. To gather accurate information about potential or actual crisis events

7. To disseminate accurate information to staff members, students, parents, and, if appropriate, the media

8. To intervene directly with staff members and students most likely to be affected

9. To increase the available supportive services for students and staff members

10. To guide students and staff members to engage in productive, appropriate responses

11. To develop interagency agreements developed in advance of a crisis, specifying
    a) Channels of communication
    b) Types of services and areas of responsibility
    c) Agreements typically are established with emergency management agencies, public safety, mental health agencies, and public health agencies

Elements of Crisis Management

The elements of crisis management in schools should include the following:

1. **Policy and Leadership** – Policy provides both a foundation and a framework for action. The chances of effectively managing a crisis are increased with a school district level crisis plan and with individual school crisis plans which operate within the framework of the school district plan but are tailored to the conditions and resources of the individual school. Leaders who understand and participate in the development of the crisis plan are necessary to ensure relevancy and effectiveness of the crisis plan as well as the appropriate implementation of the crisis plan, including maintenance of preparedness and response. School district policies typically include the following elements:

   a. Definition of crisis

   b. Definition of prevention, intervention, and recovery

   c. Development of a district-wide crisis team and a plan with all elements of crisis planning and response

Planning for Schools and Centers

d. A requirement that each school establishes a crisis management team, including guidelines on the makeup of and the responsibility of the school crisis management team

e. Development of a school site crisis management plan

f. Specifications for issues to be addressed in the district-wide and school crisis management plans include designation of chain of command, development of protocols for management of specific types of crises, coordination of communications, provisions for support services, staff members in-service training, and periodic review of the plan

g. Guidelines for working with local emergency management, public safety, mental health, public health and other agencies to coordinate a critical incident management plan

2. **Crisis Response Team** – A Crisis Response Team can be a highly effective organizational unit for dealing and preparing for a variety of crises. Such teams can operate at three levels: individual school, school district office, and community. Well-functioning teams at each level provide a crisis plan

Planning for Schools and Centers

and implementation network that can support action whenever crises arise.

3. **School District Office Crisis Management Plan** – A school district that is prepared for a wide variety of potential and active crises is in a good position to make appropriate and timely decisions if a crisis is imminent or during a crisis. The crisis plan should address strategies to gather information before, during and after a crisis. Additionally, the crisis plan should enumerate the responsibilities and roles of school district office staff members as part of the overall coordinated plan, including communication protocols, resources allocation protocols, and recovery protocols. It is important to include in the communication plans a method to communicate with every school in the school district, even if the crisis does not involve each school. A crisis will become known through the news media or through other sources and it is important for each school leader to understand the nature of the crisis in order to maintain control and preempt rumors in his or her school.

4. **School Crisis Management Plan** – A school that is prepared before a crisis occurs will be much more likely to deal with students and staff members effectively during and after a crisis. The crisis plan should be designed to result in a differentiated,

coordinated response to crises such as severe weather, community disaster, the death of a student or teacher, an in-school emergency, etc. The crisis plan should try to encompass as many possible crisis scenarios as possible. Too many times, crisis plans are too narrow and thereby focus only on a few possible crisis events.

5. **Critical Incident Management Plan -** A critical incident management plan focuses more narrowly on situations that involve imminent danger to life and limb and require a coordinated interagency response involving local emergency management, public safety, and public health resources.

6. **Training for Preparedness** – Preparation for and response to crises rely on people understanding policies and procedures and knowing what they are to do during a crisis and while preparing for an imminent crisis or possible crisis. These are best achieved through training. Maintaining preparedness is an ongoing process which involves debriefing following crises and following crisis response practices, periodic review, updating protocols, table-top (practice) exercises, and ongoing training.

7. **Communications** – Before, during, and after a
    crisis effective communication is essential within
    the school district, with parents and the community
    at large, and with the news media. Effective
    communication can speed the restoration of
    equilibrium and prevent uncontrolled and inaccurate
    rumors.   Poor communication (i.e., lack of
    communication, incorrect information, etc.) can
    make a disruptive crisis situation much worse by
    prolonging the effects of the crisis and delaying the
    return to normalcy.

Example of School District Policies and Procedures
Crisis Management Plan

Definitions

1. "Crisis incidents" include but are not limited to situations involving natural disasters, fire, use of weapons/explosives, intruders, epidemic, pandemic, student violence, etc. Such incidents typically require an interagency response involving law enforcement, emergency services agencies, mental health, and public health. At the school level, the school principal has the authority to determine if an incident or event meets the definition of a crisis and when to convene the local school crisis management team and/or ask for assistance from the districtwide crisis management team or activate the crisis plan.

2. The individual school crisis management plan is a written plan with the explicit intent to protect and sustain life, reduce emotional trauma, assist in emotional recovery from trauma, minimize personal injury and/or damage to the facility, stabilize the school environment and recognize potential hazards.

Crisis Management Team

District-wide and school crisis management teams should be established.

1. Membership: The crisis team should consist of an immediately accessible core group of staff members that have the knowledge and skills to plan for and act during any crisis. As needed, local emergency management, law enforcement, community mental health, public health, and public safety representatives should be asked to consult with the crisis team for planning and response needs. A roster of team members should be available at all times with updated communication information.

2. Purposes: The crisis management team should implement and adapt appropriate action from the crisis management plan to address the potential, imminent, and active crisis and the specific circumstances of a crisis. Roles and responsibilities of team members and consultants should be established in the written crisis management plan.

Crisis Management Plan

Each crisis management plan should include provisions for preparation and planning, intervention and response, and post-emergency activities, including the establishment or designation of the following:

1. Develop explicit procedures for crisis prevention, intervention, and response

2. Develop crisis coordination and central command post, and a local school command post if the crisis is isolated to one school

3. Chain of command should be established

4. Identify at the school district office level or at the local school level a spokesperson to the media. This person is responsible for gathering and confirming all pertinent information about the crisis and for informing the school district superintendent prior to any media release. The spokesperson will also designate a media reception area when deemed appropriate.

5. A network of key communicators should be developed. It is the responsibility of key individuals to convey approved information to others within the school or school district. This

network may include phone or text message trees to notify staff members of emergency preparations or incidents and special meetings which may occur before, during or after a crisis. It may also include staff members to support groups such as students, staff members, and parents.

6. Communication plan within the school district and communication with the community is essential. The best means of communication may depend on the type and nature of the crisis. However, a crisis plan should provide a method for communicating with parents and staff members as soon as possible. Well-informed representatives should be ready to communicate immediately. Prearranged communication modalities should be utilized to convey important information, such as through internal methods and, when appropriate, to the local news media to announce the circumstances of the crisis and other pertinent information, like the closure of schools. To ensure accuracy and avoid rumors, information to students and staff members must come directly from internal memoranda or statements written specifically for that purpose and approved by the principal or school district office. When appropriate, information about a crisis is best given to

students in class by a teacher so they can ask questions of a person they know. Questions from parents should also be addressed with accuracy while keeping in mind the FERPA restrictions on identifying students to a third party.

7. Arrangements should be made for support services and communications for school-based crises. Crisis management team should be designated to contact the school district office and to contact, as needed, other community resources such as mental health services, law enforcement, public safety and/or public health. The school district office should arrange for assistance, as needed, for additional school psychologists, school social workers, and guidance counselors even if nearby school districts need to be contacted to provide additional resources. School arrangements should include the designation of meeting spaces, provisions to request on-call services to meet unexpected demand, and provisions for long-term follow-up.

8. When a crisis has been contained and managed there should be plans on how to bring closure to the crisis and begin the recovery process. This activity will vary depending on the crisis, but it

is imperative to recognize officially the end of the crisis and the beginning of the recovery process.

9. Evaluation of the crisis plan response should start as soon as possible after the crisis has ended. Response to each crisis event should be reviewed in detail and evaluated.

Critical Incident Management Plan

1. A critical incident management plan should be developed in accordance with a Joint Memorandum of Understanding executed between the school district and leaders from law enforcement, public safety, public health, and mental health.

2. Specific school procedures should reflect utilization of an incident command center protocol and specify the key school-based procedures and methods of communication.

Crisis Management Training

The crisis management plan, including procedures for the identification of potential threats, should be reviewed annually with the school district office and local school staff members and shared with all staff members at the school district office and schools. Schools should be encouraged to provide additional in-service training on specific crisis-related topics such as intruders, multiple injuries, community health emergencies, etc.

School Safety Mandates and Requirements

Many states have enacted legislation to address school safety and crisis management issues and are requiring schools to develop crisis management procedures, often in the format of school safety plans. For example, in Georgia, *the Official Code of Georgia 20-2-1185 - School Safety Plans* requires every public school to develop a safe school plan based on crisis prevention and management.

> *Every public school shall prepare a school safety plan to help curb the growing incidence of violence in schools, to respond effectively to such incidents, and to provide a safe learning environment for Georgia's children, teachers, and other staff members. The plan shall address: natural disasters, hazardous materials or radiological accidents, acts of violence, and acts of terrorism. School safety*

Planning for Schools and Centers

plans shall be updated annually and submitted to the local emergency management agency. The Georgia Emergency Management Agency (GEMA) shall provide training and technical assistance to public school systems (crisis response team development, site surveys and safety audits, crisis management planning, exercise design, safe school planning, emergency operations planning, search and seizure, bomb threat management and model school safety plans.

School districts should ensure that its crisis management plan meets the requirements of relevant state laws and local emergency management policies or ordinances.

Leadership in Crisis Management Planning

Leadership at the school district office level is critical to the successful management of and prevention of crises. School district staff members should support, participate in and encourage the development of crisis planning district-wide and in individual schools. School district office staff members should encourage prevention strategies, as well. When a crisis occurs, the school district office staff members must be prepared to assist in many areas while allowing school staff members to deal with the immediate needs of students, staff members, and parents.

Crisis Response Designations:

1. Senior Management

2. Public Relations/Media

3. Student Support Services

4. Facilities Services

5. Transportation

6. Technology/Information Services

7. Instruction

8. Finance

9. Human Resources

Planning for Schools and Centers

10. Operational Support

11. School Nurses

12. Public Safety

Roles and Responsibilities

The school district office functions should be delineated in the crisis planning process. In large school districts, the roles in crisis planning and response may be more clearly defined because of the scope of responsibilities and logistical needs of several schools, centers, students, teachers, and resources. School district office staff members in small school districts will have multiple duties. Crisis leadership at the school level is equally important because oftentimes critical decisions must be made quickly. For any size school district and school, the roles and responsibilities in crisis planning are essential.

School District Level Leadership Functions
Senior Management (Superintendent and Central Management Staff members)

1. Directs all operations of the school district in the management of the crisis.

2. Gathers information from all aspects of the crisis for use in making appropriate decisions about the management of the crisis.

3. Assesses the immediate situation and assign tasks based on the overall needs for managing the crisis.

4. Stays in contact with the leaders of public health, emergency service agencies, law enforcement agencies working the emergency, as well as mental health and others as determined by the nature of the crisis.

5. Develops, reviews, and authorizes the release of information to the public and news media.

6. Actives the reunification sites in case students and staff members have to be evacuated from the school. Confirms that staff members are present at the reunification site along with law enforcement to maintain order, provide safety for students and staff

members, and ensure that students and staff members are reunited with their families.

7. Keeps the local school board and other local officials informed of the status of the crisis, the response to the crisis, and the impact on schools and possibly the community.

8. Invites state and local officials to coordinate assistance and to gather information.

9. Alerts local hospitals to the possibility of casualties and reports immediately to the local hospital if students or adults are being sent to the hospitals for treatment. If more than one hospital is admitting students or adults, the leaders must coordinate the communication among those hospitals and the school district. Assigns and directs other division staff members to assist at those hospitals.

10. Coordinates communication with the hospital and parents.

11. If and when possible, meets and talks with the parents of students and spouses of staff members who have been impacted directly by the crisis.

12. Establishes and maintains lines of communication between the district and the crisis site staff

members. During an off-campus crisis line of communications must be established for the involved school. Such lines of communication may also include the need for couriers if communication systems are inoperable or unavailable.

13. Communicates with all schools in the district during the crisis period.

14. Allocates assets and resources (persons and materials) to crisis sites for specific needs. This may include the assignment of staff members from other school or community sites such as community emergency shelters. If a crisis is imminent, assets and resources should be staged (put into position for quick allocation).

15. Identifies and when appropriate and necessary authorizes the immediate purchase of outside services and materials needed for the management of crisis situations.

16. Coordinates all services and personnel necessary to reopen schools.

17. Coordinates debriefing sessions after the crisis.

Student Services (Support such as School Nurses, Counselors, etc.)

1. Implements plan for the crisis and coordinates student support personnel from other schools to assist, as needed.

2. Maintains an active file of support agencies within the community including the names of contact person(s) and a rapid communication protocol. The contact names should be periodically updated and verified, and the communication methods should be routinely tested.

3. Creates letters (approved by school district office) to notify parents of continuing care that is available to students after the crisis. Available post-crisis care for students should include local support agencies, as well as school-based care.

4. Develops information sheet for parents, teachers, and others. The information should include topics such as the impact of crises on students, signs of stress (including how to recognize post-traumatic stress disorder), how to talk to children about a crisis, how to regain emotional equilibrium, etc.

5. Assists with planning and conducting parent/community meetings for information

dissemination and post-event activities and participates in district website information development.

6. Maintains follow-up communications and records on students and staff members that are referred to community-based support services, such as mental health centers, and coordinates well-check services when students and staff members return to school.

7. Assists in the coordination of debriefings with staff members after a crisis.

8. Makes recommendations to leadership regarding the restarting of school and schedule of activities for the crisis recovery phase.

Public Relations/Communications

(This critical function should be handled by someone who has had training on communications. If no one in the school district has communications training then at least two staff members should receive communication training as soon as possible.)

1. Collects and disseminates information to the news media. The staff member should consider news media reporting deadlines, the need for information accuracy, and other issues related to the news media and accurate reporting of the crisis, as well as the school district's response to the crisis.

2. Plans and coordinates press conferences - determines the location for the news media to gather, determines who will speak to the news media, and determines if news media questions will be answered.

3. Quickly disseminates information to the news media and parents when students and staff members are evacuated to a reunification site.

4. Creates and disseminates press releases (press releases should always be proofed by several staff members).

5. Arranges interviews for the news media with key school and district staff members who are involved in the crisis or who act as spokespersons for the district.

6. Acts as a liaison between the news media and school district staff members whose attention must be focused on the immediate problems of managing the crisis without constant interruptions.

7. Responds quickly to rumors through the dissemination of accurate information, and, when necessary, should quickly counter incorrect information or rumors – a timely response to rumors and incorrect information is critically important to control the crisis situation.

8. Organizes a network of key people within the community through which accurate information can be disseminated.

9. Respects FERPA requirements as well as the Freedom of Information Act and provides appropriate information to the news media based on those requirements.

10. Plans and coordinates the use of the district's website, cable television channel (if available) and social media to share and update information.

11. Coordinates development of information to be shared with school and district staff members during and after the crisis.

12. Establishes and maintains records of all communications during and after the crisis.

13. Coordinates a post-crisis debriefing on the communications component of the crisis management plan.

Facilities Services

1. Coordinates with transportation coordinator as needed.

2. Coordinates the crisis plan section that addresses imminent and actual power loss and includes the local power company providers in the planning process. Obtains and directs the placement of generators when power must be restored for a temporary period. Ensures that the power supplier is aware of the power disruption.

3. Coordinates the crisis plan section that addresses the imminent and actual loss of water and sewer and includes the local water authority in the planning process. Coordinates and directs the acquisition and

distribution of water when there is a disruption of water and sewer services. Ensures that the water and sewer agency is aware of the disruption of services.

4. Prepares and maintains accessible information for quick reference that includes school floor plans, architectural school floor plans, emergency shutdown systems schema, campus grounds maps, resources, material assets, etc.

5. Communicates with community agencies as emergency facility services are needed.

6. When appropriate and necessary, arranges for the delivery of outside services and materials needed for the management of the crisis.

7. Plans and initiates arrangements for food and/or plan for the disruption of food services or supplies to schools.

8. Participates in school district crisis debriefings.

9. Coordinates the inspection of the school with local emergency and health authorities before a school is reopened.

Transportation

1. Establishes the development of the section of the crisis plan that addresses transportation issues and response. Maintains and updates school district protocol for crisis transportation issues, including crisis-quick evacuations and alternative transportation routes.

2. Develops and implements a transportation plan to get bus drivers to their buses when needed to reach schools for crisis-quick evacuations.

3. Establishes and maintains plans for the crisis transport of students and staff members to predetermined alternate sites or schools for reunification.

4. Coordinates crisis transportation plans with local law enforcement personnel, as appropriate.

Technology/Information Services Role

1. Participates in the development of the crisis plan. Coordinates use of technology during a crisis.

2. Assists in establishment/maintenance of crisis communications networks.

3. Assists in obtaining needed student and staff member information and any facilities or resource data from the computer/data files.

4. Prepares and maintain a crisis access file that contains floor plans, telephone line locations, computer locations, and other communications equipment.

5. Establishes and maintains computer communication with the school district office and with other agency's communications systems.

6. Establishes and maintains laptops, notebook or other mobile computers with access to student and staff members database, digital floor plans, resources, transportation routes, etc.

7. With an imminent and actual crisis, provides school district staff members with updates on the status of the technology systems.

Planning for Schools and Centers

Example of School District Crisis Communication Roster

(Some staff members will have multiple roles, and it highly recommended that these names and contact information be available from a secure remote and mobile devices.)

Position/Role /Name /E-mail /Text Message/Work Phone /Fax /Home Phone/Cell Phone

1. Superintendent (or designee)

2. Assistant Superintendent

3. Facilities Liaison

4. Human Resources

5. Information Technology

6. Media Liaison

7. Community Relations

8. Safety /Security Liaison

9. Student Services

10. Superintendent

11. Transportation

12. Community or Agency Liaison

13. Other specialized

School-Level Leadership Functions

The leadership of the school principal is crucial for effective crisis management. As the highest level executive in the school, the principal bears responsibility for decisions and activities. The following is a list of school leadership functions in preparing for crisis management leadership.

1. Review district-wide policies related to crisis management, including any interagency agreements. Gain a clear understanding of the channels of communication, lines of authority, and roles and responsibilities of both school district and community agency personnel.

2. Establish a school crisis team and work with them to develop a school crisis plan that includes basic principles of crisis response as well as sections that are tailored to the school's unique needs.

3. Establish a clear chain of command within the school. Clearly, designate who is in charge in case

of a crisis when the principal is away from the school.

4. Make a point of the meeting, in advance of a crisis, with local law enforcement, emergency first responders, and public health officials who will respond to a crisis. Consult with them in developing the school's crisis plan and maintain the collaborative relationships.

5. Become thoroughly familiar with the school and grounds, including the mechanical infrastructure, as well as the local community layout and assets as well as possible impediments, such as circumstances and features of the community, roads, topography that may disrupt a crisis evacuation of the school.

6. Ensure that all staff members understand the school's crisis management plan and particularly their specific responsibilities in the event of a crisis.

7. Prepare students to assume an appropriate role by enlisting their vigilance and conducting practice drills.

8. Assure parents and the community that the school has a crisis plan in place.

Planning for Schools and Centers

Example of School Level Crisis Communication Roster
(Some staff members will have multiple roles, and it highly recommended that these names and contact information be available from secure remote and mobile devices.)

Position /Name /E-mail /Text Message/Work Phone /Home Phone /Cell Phone

1. Principal

2. Assistant Principal*

3. Team Coordinator

4. Guidance Director**

5. School Secretary

6. School Psychologist

7. School Resource Officer

8. School Social Worker

9. School Nurse

10. Teacher/Counselor

11. Teacher/Counselor

12. Custodian /Facilities

Planning for Schools and Centers

13. Transportation

14. Food

15. Service

16. Others

17. Designated an alternative person in the absence of the Principal

18. Designated an alternative person in the absence of the Crisis Response Team Coordinator.

School District Crisis Response Team

A crisis response team can be a highly effective organizational unit for dealing with a variety of crises such as accidents, intruders, suicides, incidents of violence, weather emergencies, etc. Crisis response teams in a school district can operate at three levels: (1) individual school, (2) school district, and (3) community. Well-functioning crisis response teams at each level provide a network capable of a comprehensive, coordinated response and recovery.

In addition to individual school crisis response teams, the crisis network should include a crisis response team at the district school district office level. This team may include the district superintendent or designee and senior administrators in key school division areas of operation. The school district office crisis team consults with emergency management, law enforcement, emergency responders, mental health, public utility, and public health officials and takes the lead in developing and maintaining interagency memoranda of understanding defining interagency responses to crises. The school district office crisis network would typically have responsibility for the following:

1. Issuing critical communications and decisions

2. Overseeing and coordinating the school level teams

Planning for Schools and Centers

3. Authorizing resources for areas where they are most needed. As an example, providing more counselors to a school whose staff members may be overburdened in dealing with a crisis

4. Collecting and disseminating educational materials to schools for training crisis team members and faculty

5. Establishing a central library of materials on severe weather, sheltering, violence, suicide, and other crisis management issues for use by faculty, staff members, and students.

6. Conducting mock crisis events to practice and test the crisis management procedures

7. Preparing and maintaining information that contains communications protocols, floor plans, telephone line locations, computer locations, and other facilities essentials

8. Evaluating responses to crises

9. Establishing a community support team and encouraging input and support from its members

School Level Crisis Response Team

The school level crisis response team can be led by the principal, with an alternate leader designated to assume the leadership role in the principal's absence. In addition to teachers, the team may include guidance counselor(s), school nurse, school psychologist and/or school social worker, school secretary, and custodian. School resource officers should also serve on school crisis response teams. When school resource officers are assigned to a school, they should be consulted in the development of the school's crisis management plan and involved in responses to any crisis, especially those crises involving a violation of law or threats to the safety of students and staff members. The school nurse should take a lead role during a public health crisis. The school level crisis response team typically has responsibility for the following:

1. Establishing a written protocol for dealing with crises

2. Establishing a systematic approach for identifying, referring, and addressing a crisis (and isolating students who may pose a risk or who are at risk)

3. Orienting staff members to procedures and training to fulfill designated roles, including conducting table-tip simulations and practice drills

Planning for Schools and Centers

4. Providing information to students, staff members, and community on crisis management referral procedures

5. Providing assistance during a crisis in accordance with designated roles and providing follow-up activities

6. Conducting debriefing at the conclusion of each crisis episode to critique the effectiveness of the school's crisis management plan

7. Conducting periodic reviews and updating of the crisis management plan and conducting related updated staff members training

Duties of Members of the School Crisis Response Team

The principal coordinates and supervises crisis management activities at the school. Duties include:

1. Continuity of administration

2. Development of a comprehensive school emergency management program

3. Designation and training of a school crisis management team

4. Designation and training of teachers on roles and responsibilities during a crisis

5. Designation of a command post (may be changed by responsible county public safety officials)

6. Monitor developing situations (i.e., weather conditions, an epidemic, incidents in the community that may impact the school, etc.)

7. Implement procedures and measures to control access to school.

8. Communicate with district office, law enforcement, public health, etc. during a crisis

Planning for Schools and Centers

9. Coordinate use of school as public shelter for major emergencies occurring in the area

Teachers are responsible for implementing appropriate procedures to protect students. These responsibilities include:

1. Evacuation - Direct and supervise students in route to pre-designated safe areas within the school or to an off-site evacuation shelter.

2. Classroom lockdown – Conduct classroom lockdown procedures in accordance with established procedures.

3. Student accounting - Verify the location and status of students. Report to the principal or designee on the condition of any student who needs additional assistance.

4. Student assembly/holding areas - Maintain order while in student assembly/holding areas to facilitate orderly student accounting and release or transport.

5. Establish a partner system to pair teachers and classes so that some teachers can assist with other

tasks such as first aid, search, and rescue, or community relations.

6. Remain with assigned students throughout the duration of the emergency, unless otherwise assigned through a partner system or until every student has been released through the official student release process.

Assistant Principal - Tasks related to student accounting and student release.

1. Follows procedures for assessing and reporting the status of students in a crisis or any event that results in evacuation or relocation of students.

2. Provides instruction and practice to all teachers and staff members in the student assessment and reporting process.

3. Follows procedures for communication with teachers and other school staff members during a crisis.

4. During a crisis - receives reports from all teachers on the condition and location of every student, when appropriate.

5. Assigns persons to investigate reports of any students missing, injured or ill, or otherwise not in compliance with student accounting reports.

6. Implements student release procedures.

Maintenance Head - Maintenance staff members are familiar with the operations and infrastructure of the school and are responsible for the stabilization of the school, controlling access, and securing the school facilities:

1. Inventory all hazardous materials, portable and fixed equipment, and utility lines in or near the school.

2. Follow procedures for isolating hazardous areas.

3. In a crisis, survey any damage and structural stability of schools and utilities and report to the principal.

4. Search the sections of the school for students or staff members that may be confined, injured, sick.

5. Implement school access control measures.

6. Secure student evacuation sites.

7. Assist local officials in damage assessment.

8. Assist administrators in recovery procedures.

Elements of an Effective Crisis Response Team

It is critically important for members of the Crisis Response Team to work together. Individuals that do not trust each other will not be effective during a crisis and in fact, could jeopardize important aspects of the response to a crisis. Members of the Crisis Response Team should process:

1. Professional maturity and leadership skills

2. A respectful and calm demeanor during difficult times

3. A respect for details, chain of command, and organization

4. A willingness to participate in the planning, implementation, and response stages of a crisis

5. Familiarity with the climate and nature of the school and its students, staff members, and the community

6. Willingness to problem-solve cooperatively and quickly, as needed

7. An ability to anticipate and recognize multiple problems and possible consequences

8. An ability to think clearly under stress

Planning for Schools and Centers

9. Strong communication, problem-solving, and conflict resolution skills

10. A devotion to the Crisis Management Plan and willingness to provide constructive criticism

Elements of a Dysfunctional Crisis Response Team

A dysfunctional Crisis Response Team can be easily recognized, but unfortunately, it is usually after the response was inappropriate, inadequate, or a complete failure. Therefore, it is important for leaders to take note of elements that indicate that a Crisis Response Team is dysfunctional.

1. No organized, functional crisis plan has been developed that includes all elements of an appropriate response or does not include clear delineation of Crisis Response Team member roles and responsibilities

2. Team members are inflexible and didactic

3. The crisis plan is outdated

4. Team member roles and responsibilities are unclear

5. Leadership of the team has not been clarified

6. No clearly delineated chain of command has been established

7. Team members speak to the news media without a unified voice

8. Team members respond to a crisis independent of the crisis plan

9. Team members are involved in protecting their own "turf"

10. Team members participate in spreading rumors or unconfirmed potentially inflammatory information

11. Team members share confidential information with third parties

12. Team members withhold important information from colleagues

Community Crisis Response Support Network

The school district crisis network should include community agencies and organizations such as emergency management, mental health, public safety, public health, public utilities, and social services that can be instrumental in responding to a crisis and restoring equilibrium following crisis events. School districts should maintain regular contact with community agencies and organizations in the community support network and invite them to participate in meetings with school and school district office crisis management teams.

Key Elements in Establishing a Crisis Management Plan

School districts and schools that are prepared before a crisis occurs will be much more likely to deal with disruption more effectively. Early chapters pointed out the various roles of leaders and other staff members in planning for a crisis and during a crisis.

Managing the Details

Moving into more detail in setting up a crisis management plan, the following activities should be considered.

1. Decide who will be in charge during a crisis.

A crucial first step in crisis management planning is to decide who will be in charge during a crisis. One person should be designated to provide leadership during crisis situations, to organize activities, and to disseminate information. Usually, the person in charge at the district level is the superintendent, or his/her designee, and at the school level, it should be the principal or assistant principal. A substitute should be identified in the event that the designated person is unavailable at the time of the crisis. It is extremely important that all staff members understand the lines of authority during a crisis.

2. Establish the Crisis Response Team.

A second important step is to recruit members for the Crisis Response Team. Typically at the district level, the Crisis Response Team is the superintendent's school district office staff members, while at the school level the Crisis Response Team consists of an administrator, nurse, psychologist, school social worker, teachers, counselors, and others with skills appropriate to the tasks to be performed, including school resource officers, when available. Sometimes forgotten, but important in crises, at the school level are the secretary/office manager, the head custodian, and bus drivers. Most, if not all, of the team members, must be present in the school full-time (or available and able to respond immediately to the school's needs). Some school districts have assigned bus drivers to full-time duties in schools, such as paraprofessionals so that a bus driver and bus will be available at all times should a crisis evacuation occur.

3. Develop clear and consistent policies and procedures.

It is absolutely critical to develop procedures that provide all staff members with clear guidelines for tasks and responsibilities during crises, which also ensures that all staff members will respond consistently in each situation. This applies to each and every staff member in the school. There should also be a quick reference sheet for the part-time or itinerant employees designating the roles during a crisis situation.

Planning for Schools and Centers

4. Provide training for the Crisis Response Team.

Training for school staff members, such as from FEMA, local emergency management, fire services, and public safety is essential. Also, local staff members such as school resources officers, school psychologists, school nurses, etc. can provide training for the crisis response team.

5. Establish a media liaison and identify suitable facilities where reporters can work and news conferences can be held.

Many school districts have a community or public relations spokesperson that receives all media requests and establishes procedures for responding to the media in times of crisis. This important component was specified in a previous chapter, but there may be a time when someone at a school has to assume this role. A person designated for this role should receive training from the school district's chief information officer (CIO) or from other agency CIO's who have experience communicating with the news media and the public in crisis situations.

6. Designated Command Post and Staging Areas

First responders involved in several of the recent school crisis situations recommend that schools and first responders plan for three distinct staging areas, in addition to the Command Post for the Incident Command Officer. Among other things, separate staging areas will prevent the press from converging upon parents or parents from standing too close to police. The staging areas are very important for safety and crowd control. The areas should be:

a. A **First Responders Staging Area** for law

   enforcement and emergency personnel

b. A **Media Staging Area** away from the school, at a location that can accommodate a large number of vehicles

c. A **Parent Staging Area** located away from the Command Post, where parents can reunite with their children

Maps of all command posts, listing each corresponding phone number, should be included in the Crisis Response Box.

7. Establish a working relationship with community mental health, emergency management, public health, public safety, and other resource groups.

To facilitate quick and collaborative responses, strong relationships with community agencies must be established prior to a crisis. As referenced previously, the development of a crisis management plan should include community agencies, but that is not enough. It is important to build a relationship with key personnel in the community agency. This is done through frequent contact and communications, such as inviting staff members from the community agencies to visit the schools and participate in school activities on a regular basis. In a crisis, knowing the people involved in the crisis gives it a face and a name, which can be critically important during difficult times.

8. Set up a communications network.

Critical information needs to be communicated as quickly as possible to those in need. The network should utilize multiple methods of communications. The importance of accurate information cannot be emphasized enough. Also, communication devices are constantly changing, some of which have not been fully tested in a crisis, such as during a large-scale power grid failure. Some school districts have through grants and through collaboration with local emergency management agencies purchased satellite phones for use when all other methods of communication fail. Satellite phone are expensive and are expensive to use, but they are worth the investment considering the conditions and circumstances of some schools and school districts.

9. Develop a plan for physical space management.

In a crisis, a district office or school may not be able to accommodate the influx of emergency staff members, parents and news media. Crisis management planning should anticipate the potential space needs and designate space for media, public safety operations, public health, parents, and others. The physical plant will dictate choices; however, it is wise to take into account access to telephones, water, restrooms, food and drink. Staff members who direct people and supervise these areas need to be identified in advance and trained.

10. Develop necessary forms and information sheets.

Develop record-keeping forms to assist in the management of crisis situations. Some materials may need to be translated for families into languages appropriate for the school community. Also, accurate and clear record-keeping is essential for resource identification, resource restoration, and possible resource compensation. Too often during the turmoil of a crisis, no records, logs, notes, invoices or other types of records are kept. The lack of documentation creates difficult situations for school districts with insurance companies and with claims to FEMA. An example of this is the horrendous damage to people and property caused by Hurricane Katrina. Many school districts used and in some places exceeded all of their local funding reserves trying to cope with the destruction of the massive storm while counting on reimbursement from FEMA or utilizing FEMA funds during the aftermath of the storm. However, due to poor recordkeeping, many of those school districts either did not receive compensation for their loss or were required to pay back FEMA for the crisis funds they used during and after the crisis.

11. Develop a plan for emergency coverage of classes.

Teachers who will play significant roles in a crisis response need to be assured that their classrooms will be covered when they are called from the classroom to assist in the crisis. The use of part-time staff members, itinerant staff members, and regular volunteers as possible sources of assistance in classroom coverage should be included in the crisis management plan.

12. Establish a system of codes to alert staff members.

Establish a system of codes to alert district office staff members and the same for school staff members as to the nature of a crisis without unduly alarming the rest of the school while gearing up for a crisis response. This is part of the effort and plan to avoid panic between and among students and staff members. The plan should consider the possibility that a crisis can occur rapidly and escalate without warning, which means that a crisis alarm system should be developed that every staff members member is aware of and that can be activated quickly and efficiently.

13. Develop a collection of readings.

It is important for the school district's media services to develop a bibliography of books or web-based resources pertinent to crisis planning, crisis staging, and crisis situations for central office staff members, school staff members, and auxiliary staff members. Such resources are valuable in assisting the school community to achieve a positive attitude about crisis planning, crisis response, and resolution and recovery.

14. Have school attorney review crisis response procedures and forms.

School districts and schools should adjust crisis planning components to comply with any liability concerns, based on recommendations of legal counsel. This should include procedures for documenting crisis activities and decision making. While this can be a sensitive matter, there are times when an administrator has to make decisions without fear of litigation, because of the urgency of the crisis. A leader cannot be hampered or paralyzed from making decisions in potentially life or death situations because of legal concerns.

15. Conduct practice "crisis alert" sessions with staff members and students.

Prepare staff members for their responsibilities in a real crisis. Practice several types of scenarios, but the most frequent and most likely to occur would include severe weather events, evacuations, and lockdowns. These practices should train students and staff members on what to expect and what to do. This greatly reduces the likelihood of panic during a crisis. Through table-top simulations and other practice sessions, staff members can become more proficient in responding to a variety of crises and it gives them the opportunity to contribute to the plan and to ask questions. It is best to avoid sensationalized simulations, particularly any activities involving students.

16. Conduct training in the school crisis response procedures at least annually and make it part of any new employee orientation.

Training in crisis response procedures is needed at least annually for staff members, with practices more frequent. Crisis response procedures should be part of new employee and volunteer orientations. Depending on unique situations or conditions at schools, more or specific in-service training sessions on crisis-related topics may be necessary.

Assessing Needs and Assigning Tasks

Crisis response teams should identify needs and match them with available resources. As a starting point, it is important to:

Identify Needs:

1. Areas of responsibility and tasks requiring attention in a crisis – this provides an opportunity to identify any unique needs in the school, such as how to evacuate students in wheelchairs or other students that are medically fragile

2. Physical space needs – this provides an opportunity to consider any unique structural or other physical features of the school that may offer assistance or create obstacles, such as an unused hallway that could allow a quick exit or a four-way hall intersection that could impede movement of students if they enter the same intersection at the same time.

3. Communication needs – this provides an opportunity to discuss the most effective means of communications, such as identifying parts of the school that are "dead zones" for cellphone or walkie-talkie usage.

Planning for Schools and Centers

Identify Resources

1. Staff members skills, particularly in responding to crises – this provides an opportunity to identify and discuss staff members member's training, previous careers, and a set of skills. Some staff members do not think their skills, experience, hobbies, or training would be useful during a crisis, but they should all be discussed to discern what skills could be utilized.

2. Physical space availability – this provides an opportunity to identify space resources, such as command center space, potential off-campus sites such as other schools, community centers, and churches, storage space for sheltering-in-place.

3. Communications capabilities in the school – this provides an opportunity to identify possible sources of communication, such as how many staff members have cell phones, are walkie-talkies distributed evenly or strategically throughout the school, could computers like tablets and notebooks be used for crisis communications, etc.

Match Needs and Resources

1. Assign responsibilities for specific activities and tasks; designate alternative staff members in the event of absences – this provides an opportunity to make sure the staff members given specific assignments are capable of performing the assignments. This discussion is critically important to avoid random assignments of critical duties to staff members who are not able or do not have the personality makeup or the skills to handle certain types of situations. It is unfair to put staff members in that predicament.

2. Identify physical spaces for specific types of activities and assign staff members to direct students and staff members to the appropriate space with supervision. This provides an opportunity to discuss the potential problems inherent in moving large numbers of students and staff members under stressful conditions. Moving people quickly, efficiently, and safely is very difficult during a crisis and should never be taken for granted. An unsupervised, unplanned movement of students and staff members can create a hazardous situation.

3. Develop a communications plan with alternative strategies – this provides an opportunity to discuss communication failures and how to create and

implements backup communication plans, such as the strategic placement of bullhorns throughout the school in case other communications devices or methods fail.

Example of School Staff Members Inventory of Skills and Experience

Check any of the following in which you have expertise or training:

Crisis Response Skills

1. First aid – name and room location:

2. Logistics – name and room location:

3. Communications – name and room location:

4. Fire Safety / Firefighting – name and room location:

5. CPR – name and room location:

6. Search & Rescue – name and room location:

7. EMT – name and room location:

8. Critical Incident Stress Debriefing – name and room location:

9. Law Enforcement – name and room location:

10. Post-traumatic Stress Training – name and room location:

Planning for Schools and Centers

11. Other (Please specify) _____ – name and room location:

(Using information gathered in the inventory above, lists such as the one below can be developed for quick reference based on needs during a crisis)

Staff members with Medical Care Skills

1. Name:

2. Location:

3. Notification Method:

4. Training/Certification:

Staff members with Communication Devices

1. Name:

2. Location:

3. Notification Method:

4. Type of device and contact information:

Bi/Multi-Lingual Staff members

1. Name:

2. Location:

3. Notification Method

4. Languages:

Staff members with Sign Language Skills

1. Name:

2. Location:

3. Notification Method:

Students Who May Need Special Assistance in a Crisis

1. Name:

2. Location (schedule of all classes):

3. Description of Assistance Needed:

4. Staff members Member Assigned to Assist Student:

5. Location of Staff members Member Assigned to Assist Student:

Staff members Who May Need Special Assistance in a Crisis

1. Name:

2. Location (schedule of all classes):

3. Description of Assistance Needed:

4. Staff members Member Assigned to Assist Staff members Member:

5. Location of Staff members Member Assigned to Assist Staff members Member:

Example of School Staff Members Assignment Roster Assignment Position/Name Operations Site(s)

Principal:

Assistant Principal (s):

Main Office:

Crisis Team Coordinator:

Alternate Coordinator:

Guidance Office:

Guidance Secretary:

Media Center:

Family Contact Guidance staff members:

School Social Worker:

Career Guidance Conference Room:

School Nurse:

Support Counseling for Students/ Staff members

Guidance staff members:

School Psychologist:

246 | P a g e

Example of Crisis Planning for Off-Campus Activities

Off-campus activities, including field trips, should follow a crisis protocol with the following information and essentials:

1. **Use name tags / personal identification** – note that these need to be worn on blouses or shirts rather than outer garments such as sweaters and coats which may be removed during bus trips. Write-bracelets might be considered for identification, particularly for younger children.

2. **A route map and itinerary should be left at the school** – school leadership and the school district transportation leadership should know the location of field trips or events and the proposed route to the location. Bus drivers should be instructed to follow the proposed route and to notify their transportation supervisor and the school if the route has to change.

3. **A manifest of riders in each bus or another vehicle should be left at the school before departure** - Students, staff members, and volunteers should travel to and return from the activity site in the same vehicle. This should be an absolute requirement because it is the only way to ensure that all students, staff members, and volunteers are accounted for. Riders should be verified against the manifest when departing from

Planning for Schools and Centers

the school or site and verified when loading for the trip back to the school.

4. **Determine who has cell phones.** It is desirable for someone in each vehicle to have a cell phone in addition to the bus radio transmitter. The cell phone numbers should be included on the manifest left at the school.

5. **Bus Emergency Kit**

   - Cell phone or other emergency communications equipment.

   - Rider roster (students, staff members, volunteers)

   - Signs to display bus numbers

   - Route maps with backup or emergency alternative routes noted

   - Route maps to hospitals and crisis reunification sites

   - Area maps

   - Pen, paper or notebooks

Planning for Schools and Centers

- Stick-on name tags (or write-bracelets for younger students)

- First aid kit

- Emergency telephone numbers list

- District office (including cell phone numbers)

- Emergency medical services phone numbers if 911 service is not available in the area

- Law enforcement (State Police)

- Incident Report Forms

A Crisis When School is Not in Session

If a school administrator or another crisis response team member is notified of a crisis when school is not in session, the following steps should be taken:

1. Institute the communication contact protocol to disseminate information to appropriate staff members and parents.

2. Notify appropriate staff members by letter, email, text or telephone with information about the incident.

3. Be alert for any collateral after-effects of the incident, such as something carrying over into the school like retribution, for example.

4. If the crisis involved possible damage to the school or otherwise may have created unsafe conditions at the school, close school until the school has been determined to be safe.

5. Use news media of other means of communicating with parents regarding whether the school will be open or closed.

Example of Incident Report Form

(Example of report to document crisis details – should be submitted to the superintendent or designee and reviewed by School District Crisis Response Team for debriefing and adjustments in the Crisis Management Plan or training)

Crises Response Team Report

Date of Report_____

School _____

Staff Member or Members Filing the Incident Report

_____

_____

Description of incident (include date, time, place)

_____

_____

Intervention/Response Activities

_____

_____

Follow-up procedures (with student, with student body [if appropriate], with staff)

_____

_____

Follow-up with parent(s)/guardian(s) of student(s) involved or community members

_____

_____

List agencies and others that provided support and assistance during the crisis

_____

_____

Assessment of school's Crisis Plan and response

_____

_____

Other Information

_____

_____

Reviewed by Principal: _____

Date: _____

Post-Crisis Incident Management and Recovery
Follow-up to Crisis Situations

The following information may be useful in the days and weeks following a crisis. Longer term follow-up procedures are also listed.

Short-term

1. Gather staff members and update them on any additional information/ procedures. Allow members opportunity to discuss feelings and reactions, with support staff members available.

2. In the case of death, provide funeral/visitation information if affected family has given permission.

3. Identify students and staff members in need of follow-up support and, in accordance with the school's crisis management plan, assign staff members to monitor vulnerable students and other staff members.

4. Coordinate any ongoing counseling support for students on campus.

5. Announce ongoing support for students with the place, time, and staff member facilitators.

6. Develop academic recovery plans, based on the nature of the crisis and duration of the crisis (NOTE: If the situation required a long-term school closure, questions may need to be directed to the state's department of education.)

Long-term Follow-up and Evaluation

1. Provide a list of suggested readings to teachers, parents, and students to aid in the recovery.

2. Write thank-you notes to out-of-school district and community resource people who provided (or are still providing) support during the crisis.

3. Some students or staff members may experience "anniversary" reactions the following month or year on the date of the crisis, or when similar crises occur that remind them of the original crisis; therefore, be alert on crisis anniversaries and holidays.

Crisis Response Team Post-Crisis Debriefing

Post-incident debriefing is a process that reviews the school's and/or school district's response to the crisis and how it may be improved.

Example of Crisis Response Team Post-Crisis Debriefing

The systematic process of debriefing should include a review of each of the following. Ask for explanations to the answers and provide opportunities for staff members to express any frustrations and fears as well as suggestions.

1. **Initial understanding of crisis**

   Was the information accurate? Was the information complete? Were there misunderstandings? Was there confusion? Ask for explanations to the answers and provide opportunities for staff members to express any frustrations, fears as well as suggestions.

2. **Initial strategies and tactics**

   Were the first steps after the crisis appropriate? What else could have been done? What worked well? What could be done differently?

3. **Results of strategies and tactics**

    Were the intended results achieved? Were there
    any unintended consequences?

4. **Obstacles encountered**

    What? Who? Why? When? How? Were obstacles
    dealt with appropriately? Can anything be done to
    prevent obstacles in the future?

5. **Staff members**

    Was appropriate staff members notified in a timely
    manner? Was staff members properly prepared to
    respond in an appropriate manner? Did staff
    members respond in an appropriate manner? Do
    staff members need additional training?

6. **Recommendations for improvement**

    What lessons were learned? Are there policies
    and/or procedures that need to be amended? Does
    communication procedures and equipment need to
    be reviewed or updated?

7. **Academic Recovery Review**

If the crisis required school closure for several days or weeks, how well did the academic recovery plan work? What was learned from implementing the academic recovery plan? What, if any, resources could have been better utilized? What resources should be gathered in preparation for a future crisis? Did students benefit from the academic recovery plan/strategies?

Maintaining Crisis Preparedness Following a Crisis

It is critically important for schools and school districts to maintain a high level of crisis preparedness throughout the year and revisit preparedness after a crisis. Contrary to popular opinion, there is a tendency for schools that have experienced a crisis to let its preparedness condition lapse out of an unfounded belief that a crisis will not happen again and from the misplaced feeling that the students and staff members will be traumatized if there are discussions about crisis management after a crisis.

Maintaining Crisis Awareness and Preparedness

One of the most effective means of maintaining awareness and preparedness is to periodically review the Crisis Management Plan. The following is an example checklist for a review of and access to a Crisis Management Plan.

1. Print updated crisis referral information in the student handbook.

2. Print updated crisis referral information in the faculty handbook.

3. Confirm membership of Crisis Response Team, filling vacancies that have occurred.

4. Review assigned roles and responsibilities of team members and revise, as needed.

Planning for Schools and Centers

5. Review overall Crisis Management Plan and update in light of changes in conditions and/or resources at the school or in the community.

6. Review Critical Incident Management procedures and update in light of changes in conditions and/or resources at the school or in the community.

7. Update faculty of any changes in Crisis Response Team membership and procedures including identification/intervention referral, for crisis response, critical incident response, and post-event.

8. Include a review of Crisis Management Plan and related procedures in new staff members orientation.

9. Hold a staff meeting on the Crisis Management Plan and provide training in related topics on a regular basis.

10. Provide training locally or from the local emergency management agency and/or the state emergency management agency on prevention and crisis management.

Crisis Response Box

The concept of a Crisis Response Box is for the purpose of responding to a crisis by housing all essential information and guidelines in one place and in a container that is mobile or stored digitally so it can be retrieved remotely. Some school districts are now loading all of the following information onto secured laptop or notebook computers or in secured "cloud" technology that can be retrieved through smartphones, laptops, or digital notebooks. The Crisis Response Box should contain the following items.

Aerial Photographs of Campus

An aerial perspective of the campus and the surrounding area is very helpful to all agencies involved in a critical incident, including police, fire, and paramedic personnel. Local municipalities may be able to provide an aerial photo of schools and surrounding campus, and aerial photographs of school campuses may be download from a source such as Google Earth (check the date of the aerial photograph).

Campus Layout

It is important to maintain current, accurate blueprints, classroom layouts and floor plans of the school and grounds, including information about main leads for water, gas, electricity, cable, telephone, alarm and sprinkler systems, hazardous materials (e.g. science labs, storage areas, boiler room) location, elevators and entrances. This information is extremely helpful, especially during a "shelter-in-place" situation when students are locked in a classroom and/or other locations in the school. Information should be available on the layout of the school, including room numbers and whether or not there is a phone, intercom, cable television, e-mail, computers or cell phones in the classroom. On the campus layout diagram, it is also helpful to highlight areas that could pose a possible threat, such as the chemistry laboratory, biology laboratory or any welding and wood shop areas that could also become a location for explosions or that contain items that could be used as weapons. These items can be designated by color or symbol on the campus layout.

Blueprint of School Schools

Architectural blueprints of the school are important to first responders such as a SWAT team and fire department because they provide additional -- and more detailed – information than the simple classroom layout diagram. It is also helpful to show the location of the fire alarm turn-off, sprinkler system turn-off, utility shut-off valves, cable television shut-off and first aid supply boxes. This information may be critical, especially in the event of a bomb threat, intruder or unidentified odor or smoke. The plant manager for the school site and the principal and assistant principal should have quick access to the blueprints in a digital format and/or hard copy format. Grounds and maintenance staff members and assistant principals of the school should be familiar with these blueprints and their location.

Staff members Member Roster

A staff member roster should go into the Crisis Response Box. Teachers' names on the classroom layout diagram can help first responders. If this is not possible, each teacher's name should be matched with his or her classroom and a note should be included that denotes whether or not each teacher has a cell or land phone. This roster should identify any staff member with special medical needs (e.g., diabetes) who will require medications during a prolonged period and those with a disability who

Planning for Schools and Centers

may require assistance in an evacuation. Someone in the front office should be assigned to pick up the visitor/volunteer/substitute teacher list in the event of a critical incident.

Keys or Card Access

The Crisis Response Box should also contain a master key and an extra set of keys. The keys must be clearly tagged. The keys should be placed in a locked container within the box to assure added security in case the box should end up in the wrong hands. Some schools have found it advantageous to keep the master key in a Key Box (rapid entry system) outside of the school. This is a secure metal box that can easily be accessed by a code or a key without having to enter the school. This can prove especially helpful when it is not safe to enter the school or if a first responder needs access to the school. Further information on a Key Box can be obtained from the local fire department. School districts and schools with a card access system should have a very specific card distribution system protocol that includes procedures for card distribution, for appropriate use of the cards, for card retrieval when an employee leaves the school or school district, and for deactivation of the card system. The distribution system description should be in the Crisis Response Box.

As school districts move to keyless and card-less access to schools as well as digital access mechanisms, they should develop access procedures for crisis situations, as well as develop safeguards that signal when the digital system or systems have been compromised or fail.

Fire Alarm Turn-off Procedures

One of the lessons learned from Columbine was to make it easier to turn off the alarm. The loud alarm made it very difficult for first responders to hear instructions and directions. It took considerable time before someone who knew how to turn it off was able to do so. School officials learned that they cannot assume that the person who knows how to turn off the alarm will be logistically able to do so. If that person is inside the school, he or she might not be able to get to the shutoff mechanism; if that person is outside, it is possible that he or she might not be able to safely re-enter the school. As a result, a number of people need to know how to shut off the alarm, or it should be a system that can shut off remotely.

Sprinkler System Turn-off Procedures

Sprinkler systems may activate during a crisis. During the incident at Columbine, no one was readily available who knew how to immediately turn off the sprinkler system. As a result, hallways quickly filled with water, making it difficult for students to evacuate the school. In some places, the water reached dangerous levels in proximity to the electrical outlets -- water reaching such outlets could have caused many more injuries and possibly additional deaths. The Crisis Response Box should include information on where shutoff valves are located in the school and the shutoff procedures.

Utility Shutoff Valves

Shutoff and access points of all utilities -- gas, electric and water – need to be clearly identified and their locations listed on the campus layout and floor plans so they can be quickly shut off in a crisis. If there is not a fire, the water should be shut off immediately to prevent flooding from the sprinkler system. Unless open electric or gas lines pose an immediate threat to life, the decision on whether to shut off these lines should be made by the Incident Command Officer or first responders. The Crisis Response Box needs to include this information on where shutoff valves are located in the school and the shut-off procedures.

Cable Television, Satellite, Digital Feed Shut-off

If a school has a feed for an internal surveillance system or classroom monitors, using cable, satellite or a digital format, school staff members should be prepared to disable the system in a crisis, particularly during an intruder situation when the intruder has taken over much of the school. Several law enforcement officers involved in nationally televised shootings recommend that the feed is shut off so that any intruders on the inside will not be able to view the whereabouts of the SWAT team by tuning into a live feed on the school's monitors. If there is an intruder in the school, the decision to utilize or disable the system should be made by the first responders. On the other hand, in some other situations, the system can be helpful to provide those who are sheltered-in-place with up-to-date information or if the system can be accessed by first responders to view the location of intruders or to find the location of students and staff members. The Crisis Response Box needs to include this information.

Student and Staff members Member Photographs

Student and staff member photos can help in the essential task of identifying students injured, missing or deceased. Staff members should have access to the Crisis Response Box for copies of student and staff members member photo IDs, the most recent school yearbook (along with the additional photos of the newest incoming class) or a digitally stored file of student and staff members member photographs. If photos are digital, it could assist first responders if the photos were available on a CD, which should be included in the Crisis Response Box. Many law enforcement agencies and other first responders bring laptops to the scene and can thereby gain instant access to such photos, print them out, make copies and distribute them to other first responders. This could be critically important to locate and account for every student and staff member. *Be very mindful of FERPA restrictions on sharing student information.*

Incident Command System (ICS) Key Responders' Contact Information

Names and phone numbers for all team participants involved in coordinating with the local emergency response system should be in the Crisis Response Box. Also, the names, phone numbers, email addresses, and text message contacts of other key staff members should be included.

Emergency Resource List

A list of individuals and organizations that can assist in a crisis should be prepared and included in the Crisis Response Box so that designated staff members can immediately begin to make phone calls to those on the list. Please note that any staff members member or volunteer enlisted to make the response phones to agencies and other community services must be pre-screened and receive training. This is an example of a list of contact phone numbers that should be in the Crisis Response Box.

1. Local emergency management

2. State emergency management

3. Local law enforcement

4. Local fire and rescue

Planning for Schools and Centers

5. Community counselors (A cadre of trained crisis intervention counselors should be identified to provide mental health a first aid during and following the crisis, including counselors from mental health services)

6. Local public health department

7. Local television and radio channels

8. National Organization for Victim Assistance (NOVA)

9. Parent representative(s) (The parent representatives should be trained to help fellow parents receive information, answer questions and maintain calm at the Parent Staging Area.)

Map of Streets

Crisis response planners need to review the traffic patterns and intersections that could be affected by a major crisis. Through this process, sites and locations can be identified where parents or guardians can retrieve their children after an incident. Also, this will assist in the identification and anticipation of traffic safety issues that school transportation staff members and other staff members and law enforcement will have to consider when directing students and staff members to safe areas. The map

Planning for Schools and Centers

should be available digitally and/or hard copies for emergency responders and staff members. An emergency traffic plan should be developed that is capable of protecting emergency response routes and accommodating traffic and parking needs for parents, students, emergency responders and the news media. The map should illustrate these planned routes as well as:

1. The streets surrounding the school

2. Intersections near the school

3. Vacant lots near the school

4. Possible relocation sites and schools for students and staff members

5. Location of major utilities near the routes

6. Possible hazards in or near the routes

Evacuation Routes and Reunification Sites

Maps with evacuation and alternate evacuation routes along with reunification and secondary reunification sites should be stored in the Crisis Response Box. The maps will indicate which routes students and staff members will likely follow and the destination they are seeking. This is important in order to identify them, or, if they are missing, to determine where along the route they might be

Planning for Schools and Centers

found. Be aware, however, that during some crisis the evacuation routes may have to be altered. That is why it is critically important to have alternate routes and reunification sites. All classrooms at Columbine, for example, had evacuation plans, but with two students shooting throughout the entire school, evacuating the school was itself a dangerous venture. In the Jonesboro, Arkansas incident, two boys opened fire while students evacuated the school during a false fire alarm. Other factors may alter evacuation routes. In a chemical spill, for instance, how the winds are blowing will determine where to evacuate. Thus, it is important to have at least two predetermined evacuation routes identified and included in the Crisis Response Box.

Designated Command Post and Staging Areas

First responders involved in several of the recent school crisis situations recommend that schools and first responders plan for three distinct staging areas, in addition to the Command Post for the Incident Command Officer: first responders' staging area; news media staging area; and parent staging area. The staging areas prevent chaos and allow the school to keep track of students and staff members, as well as providing access to injured students. Maps of all command posts and staging areas listing each corresponding phone number and other contact information should be included in the Crisis Response Box.

Planning for Schools and Centers

Student Disposition Forms and Crisis Data Cards

Because of the possibility of hundreds of parents descending upon a school to reunite with their children while the school is trying to account for each student's whereabouts, schools should have forms to keep track of which students have been released and to whom: parents, relatives, emergency personnel or the hospital. It is suggested that a set of release forms (enough to cover the entire school census) be stored in the Crisis Response Box, or a laptop or other digital means of collecting and storing this information. Additionally, if possible, it is helpful to have a set of student crisis data cards included in the Crisis Response Box or the same information in a digital format. Having all the data stored on a CD, flash drive or laptop/notebook is an accessible way of containing and accessing the information. Crisis information can also be stored, updated and retrieved electronically either from the school or a remote site.

Student Attendance Roster

One of the most difficult challenges in a crisis is accounting for all students. Teachers should have a readily accessible listing of all pupils in their charge, either in a written format or in an accessible digital format. Teachers should also be instructed to take their classroom attendance list (printed or digital) with them during an evacuation. A system should be developed to retrieve these lists from teachers when it is safe and feasible. Someone should be assigned to place that day's attendance roster into the Crisis Response Box or digitally **each morning**. This critical information can then be available for school staff members and first responders during an emergency. It is not enough to simply have the classroom rosters; first responders need to know which students were actually in school at the time of the crisis. Some schools store all student attendance and information data digitally, thus making remote access to the data possible.

Inventory of Staff members Resources

The staff member inventory of special skills, experiences and training should be included in the Crisis Response Box. Experience, skills, and training in the following areas could offer needed assistance: medical and triage experience, bilingual capabilities, grief counseling background, search and rescue training, hostage negotiations, first aid/CPR certification and volunteer firefighter or reserve police officer/deputy.

List of Students and Staff members with Special Needs

A list should also be included in the Crisis Response Box that identifies those students and staff members who need special assistance (e.g., blind and deaf students and those who need wheelchairs, crutches, and braces) and/or with special medical needs (e.g., diabetes) that will require medications during a prolonged period.

First Aid Supplies Location

Sets of first aid supplies should be located throughout the campus. Storage location maps should be included in the Crisis Response box.

Crisis First Aid Supplies

The FBI Academy recommends that schools be aware of information from the *Lessons Learned Summit* regarding first aid supplies. In the Jonesboro, Arkansas shooting, large bins of first aid supplies were readily accessible on the school grounds and are credited with saving two children's lives and preventing others from going into shock. First aid supplies were situated inside and outside of the school in anticipation of an earthquake because the school property is located on a fault line. The accessibility of these supplies proved to be lifesaving. Some schools have stationed first aid boxes in every classroom with basic emergency aid instructions to treat various injuries. Some schools have created Medical Go Kits that include standard First Aid supplies and located throughout the school and assigned to specified staff members. This information should be included in the Crisis Response Box.

Reference Information Checklist for Crisis Response Maps

- ✓ Streets surrounding school
- ✓ Intersections near school
- ✓ Vacant lots
- ✓ Possible evacuation hazards or impediments
- ✓ Location of nearby schools that can be used for temporary housing (e.g., community gym, church, auditorium, etc.)

Campus Layout and Blueprint of School
- ✓ Room numbers, phone numbers, computers, e-mail, cable TV
- ✓ Threat areas (e.g., chemistry and biology labs, shops, gasoline storage areas, boiler rooms)

Teacher/Staff members Member Roster
- ✓ Room and cell phone numbers
- ✓ Staff members directory
- ✓ Copy of employee photo Identifies

Fire Alarm Turn-off Procedures
- ✓ How and where located

Sprinkler System Turn-off Procedures
- ✓ How and where located

Utility Shut-off Valves
- ✓ Electric
- ✓ Gas
- ✓ Water
- ✓ Where and how to shut off

Gas Line and Utility Lines Lay-Out
- ✓ This information can be provided by school district service center or local utility departments

First Aid Supplies
- ✓ Location and how to access

Designated Command Posts
- ✓ Identify Area for Law Enforcement, Emergency Personnel
- ✓ Receiving Area for Parents
- ✓ Receiving Area for Press

Cable Television or Surveillance Camera Shut-off or Monitoring
- ✓ Identify where and how

Student and Staff members Member Photographs
- ✓ Copy of photo IDs of students
- ✓ Current yearbook

Evacuation Sites
- ✓ Maps with routes to at least two evacuation sites; should also be posted in classrooms.

Disposition Forms
- ✓ Set of forms for parents/guardians/hospitals/ER personnel to sign when a student has been released to them.

Student Attendance Roster
- ✓ Roster should be entered in the box daily
- ✓ Teachers bring their classroom attendance sheet to evacuation site

List of Students with Special Needs

- ✓ List of students with special medical needs requiring medications
- ✓ List of students with a disability requiring assistance in an evacuation
- ✓ Student emergency card data

References

1. Richards, E. P., and Rathbun, K. C. (1998). "Public Health Law." In *Maxcy-Rosenau-Last Public Health and Preventive Medicine,* ed. R. B. Wallace. Stamford, CT: Appleton and Lange.

2. Cauchemez, S., Ferguson, N.M., Wachtel, C., Tegnell. A., Saor, G., Duncan, B., and Nicoll, A. (2009). *Closure of schools during an influenza pandemic.* The Lancet, Vol. 9, 1-9.

3. McGiboney, G. (2007). *Pandemic Planning for Schools.* National Federation of Urban and Suburban School Districts Conference, Charleston, West Virginia.

4. Carlyle, Robyn Correll, *Questions About Pandemics*, Huffington Post, Aug 30, 2013.

5. *Early Warning, Timely Response: A Guide to Safe Schools*, United States Department of Education. Retrieved 2013.

6. *Crisis Management Guide*, United States Department of Defense Education. Retrieved 2014.

7. *Safe School Facilities Checklist.* (2013). National Clearinghouse for Educational Facilities.

8. *Neighborhood and Campus Facility Risk Factors.* (2009). American Clearinghouse on Educational Facilities.

9. *Multi-hazard Emergency Planning for Schools Toolkit.* (2010). Federal Emergency Management Agency.

10. *Guidelines for School Facilities.* (2000). Virginia Department of Education.

11. *Sample School Emergency Operations Plan.* (2011). Federal Emergency Management Agency.

12. *Safety and Emergency Plan.* San Francisco Unified School District.

13. State Emergency Management Agency – Safe Schools Unit

14. *Emergency Management Planning for Schools.* Seattle Public School District

15. *Planning for Emergencies.* DeKalb County School District (State)

16. Richards, E. P., and Rathbun, K. C. (1998). "Public Health Law." In *Maxcy-Rosenau-Last Public Health and Preventive Medicine,* ed. R. B. Wallace. Stamford, CT: Appleton and Lange.

17. *Community Emergencies.* California Contra Costa Health Services

18. *Interim Pre-Pandemic Planning Guidance.* Centers for Disease Control. *www.pandemicflu.gov*

19. *Planning and Preparedness.* www.flu.gov.

20. *HHS Pandemic Influenza Plan.* United States Department of Health and Human Services.

21. *World Health Organization Checklist for Influenza Preparedness Planning.* World Health Organization.

22. *CDC Resources for Pandemic Flu.* Centers for Disease Control.

23. United States Department of Education, *Pandemic Planning www.ed.gov*

Scientific References

1. Kilbourne, E.D. Influenza pandemics of the 20th century. *Emerging Infectious Diseases* 2006;12:9–14.

2. Morgridge.org/wp-content/uploads/2014/09/H1N1-fact-sheet.pdf

3. Garten, R.J.; Davis, C.T.; Russell, C.A., et al. Antigenic and genetic characteristics of swine-origin 2009 A(H1N1) influenza viruses circulating in humans. *Science* 2009;325:197–201.

4. Jhung, M.A.; Epperson, S.; Biggerstaff, M., et al. Outbreak of variant influenza A (H3N2v) virus in the United States. *Clinical Infectious Diseases* 2013;57:1703–12.

5. Uyeki, T.M. Global epidemiology of human infections with highly pathogenic avian influenza A (H5N1) viruses. *Respirology* 2008;13(Suppl 1):S2–9.

6. CDC. Emergence of avian influenza A(H7N9) virus causing severe human illness—China, February–April 2013. *MMWR* 2013;62:366–71.

7. Gaydos, J.C.; Top, F.H.; Hodder, R.A.; and Russell, P.K. Swine influenza A outbreak, Fort Dix, New Jersey, 1976. *Emerging Infectious Diseases* 2006;12:23–8.

8. US Department of Health and Human Services. 2009
H1N1 influenza improvement plan. Washington, DC:
US Department of Health and Human Services; 2012.
Available at
http://www.phe.gov/Preparedness/mcm/h1n1-
retrospective/Documents/2009-h1n1-improvementplan.
pdf .

9. World Health Organization. WHO global influenza
preparedness plan: the role of WHO and
recommendations for national measures before and
during pandemics. Geneva, Switzerland: World Health
Organization; 2005.
Available at
http://www.who.int/csr/resources/publications/influenza
/WHO_CDS_CSR_GIP_2005_5.pdf.

10. US Homeland Security Council. National strategy for
pandemic influenza. Washington, DC: U.S. Homeland
Security Council; 2005.
Available at
http://www.flu.gov/professional/federal/pandemic-
influenza.pdf .

11. US Homeland Security Council. National strategy for
pandemic influenza: implementation Plan. Washington,
DC: US Homeland Security Council; 2006.
Available at

http://www.flu.gov/planning-
preparedness/federal/pandemic-influenza-
implementation.pdf.

12. US Department of Health and Human Services. Key
elements of departmental pandemic influenza
operational plans. Appendix A: pandemic intervals,
triggers, and actions. Washington, DC: US Department
of Health and Human Services; 2008. Available at
http://www.flu.gov/planning-
preparedness/federal/operationalplans.html#.

13. Trock, S.C.; Burke, S.A., and Cox, N.J. Development
of an influenza virologic risk assessment tool. *Avian
Diseases,* 2012;56:1058–61.

14. Reed, C.; Biggerstaff, M.; Finelli, L.; et al. Novel
framework for assessing epidemiologic effects of
influenza epidemics and pandemics. *Emerging
Infectious Diseases*, 2013;19:85–91.

15. World Health Organization. Pandemic influenza risk
management: WHO interim guidance. Geneva,
Switzerland: World Health Organization; 2013.
Available at
http://www.who.int/influenza/preparedness/pandemic/i
nfluenza_risk_management/en.

16. World Health Organization. Alert, response, and capacity building under the International Health Regulations (IHR). Geneva, Switzerland: World Health Organization; 2005.
Available at
http://www.who.int/ihr/procedures/pheic/en/index.html.

17. CDC. Interim pre-pandemic planning guidance: community strategy for pandemic influenza mitigation in the United States—early, targeted, layered use of non-pharmaceutical interventions. Atlanta, GA: CDC; 2007.
Available at
http://www.flu.gov/planning-preparedness/community/community_mitigation.pdf

18. Hatchett, R.J.; Mecher, C.E.; and Lipsitch, M. Public health interventions and epidemic intensity during the 1918 influenza pandemic. *National Academy of Sciences*, U S A 2007;104:7582–7.

19. Markel, H.; Lipman, H.B.; Navarro, .JA., et al. Non-pharmaceutical interventions implemented by U.S. cities during the 1918–1919 influenza pandemic. *JAMA*, 2007;298:644–54.

20. Ferguson, N.M.; Cummings, D.A.; Fraser, C.; Cajka, J.C.; Cooley, .PC.; and Burke, D.S. Strategies for mitigating an influenza pandemic. *Nature*, 2006; 442:448–52.

21. Bootsma, M.C. and Ferguson N.M. The effect of public health measures on the 1918 influenza pandemic in U.S. cities. *National Academy of Sciences*, U S A 2007;104:7588–93.

22. Davey, V.J. and Glass, R.J. Rescinding community mitigation strategies in an influenza pandemic. *Emerging Infectious Diseases*, 2008;14:365–72.

23. Barrios L.C.; Koonin L.M.; Kohl K.S.; and Cetron, M. Selecting non-pharmaceutical strategies to minimize influenza spread: the 2009 influenza A (H1N1) pandemic and beyond. *Public Health Report*, 2012;127:565–71.

Index

THE BOOK

Schools around the nation and the world face unprecedented challenges regarding public health issues. This book was written to support and encourage the development and implementation of a comprehensive pandemic plan that can also be used for epidemics. It contains protocols and procedures, including a comprehensive section on pandemic and epidemic planning and response and essential components in crisis planning. It is designed to be used as a general resource and as a training tool. It contains specific information, protocols aimed at operational functions, and it can be adapted to any type of school setting, including non-traditional school settings. In addition to being a planning guide and training manual, the book is intended to be a quick reference resource, which makes the numerous checklists and specific language valuable as an immediate aid.

THE AUTHOR

Dr. Garry McGiboney is a nationally recognized expert on school leadership, school crisis management, and crisis planning and response. He has made hundreds of presentations across the United States and is often a keynote speaker at state and national conferences. He has published over 30 professional articles and is the author of six books. Dr. McGiboney has appeared on *CNN, A&E, Discovery Channel, Public Broadcasting Service, National Public Radio, Nickelodeon Network* and many local and regional television and radio programs. He has been quoted in *Time* magazine, *Education Week, USA Today,* and many others, including the international press. Dr. McGiboney is the recipient of numerous awards, such as the NAACP Educator of the Year, National Association of School Psychologists Friend of Children Award, and many others. He was recently inducted into the University System of Georgia Hall of Fame for his career-long services to children. He has a Ph.D. from Georgia State University in psychology and administration.

EPC - EINSTAR PUBLISHING COMPANY

Planning for Schools and Centers